Communism: opposing viewpoints. Edited
by Bruno Leone. Second ed. revised.
St. Paul, Mn. Greenhaven Press, Inc.
c.1986.
216p. (The Isms: Modern doctrines and
movements).

Includes bibliographies and index.

1.Communism. I.Leone, Bruno.
II.Series.

The Isms: Modern Doctrines and Movements

Communism

Opposing Viewpoints

Other Volumes Available in the *ISMS SERIES:*

Capitalism
Feminism
Internationalism
Nationalism
Racism
Socialism

The Isms: Modern Doctrines and Movements

Communism

Opposing
Viewpoints

REVISED EDITION

Bruno Leone

Greenhaven Press
577 Shoreview Park Road
St. Paul, Minnesota 55126

Library of Congress Cataloging-in-Publication Data

Communism : opposing viewpoints.

(The Isms)
Includes bibliographies and index.
1. Communism.   I. Leone, Bruno, 1939-
II. Series.
HX72.C64   1986   335.43   86-338
ISBN 0-89908-385-4 (lib bdg.)
ISBN 0-89908-360-9 (pbk.)

Second Edition
Revised

"Congress shall make no law . . .
abridging the freedom of speech,
or of the press."

first amendment to the U.S. Constitution

The basic foundation of our democracy is the first amendment guarantee of freedom of expression. The Opposing Viewpoints books are dedicated to the concept of this basic freedom and the idea that it is more important to practice it than to enshrine it.

Contents

Why Consider Opposing Viewpoints?

"It is better to debate a question without settling it than to settle a question without debating it."

Joseph Joubert (1754-1824)

The Importance of Examining Opposing Viewpoints

The purpose of the Opposing Viewpoints books, and this book in particular, is to present balanced, and often difficult to find, opposing points of view on complex and sensitive issues.

Probably the best way to become informed is to analyze the positions of those who are regarded as experts and well studied on issues. It is important to consider every variety of opinion in an attempt to determine the truth. Opinions from the mainstream of society should be examined. But also important are opinions that are considered radical, reactionary, or minority as well as those stigmatized by some other uncomplimentary label. An important lesson of history is the eventual acceptance of many unpopular and even despised opinions. The ideas of Socrates, Jesus, and Galileo are good examples of this.

Readers will approach this book with their own opinions on the issues debated within it. However, to have a good grasp of one's own viewpoint, it is necessary to understand the arguments of those with whom one disagrees. It can be said that those who do not completely understand their adversary's point of view do not fully understand their own.

A persuasive case for considering opposing viewpoints has been presented by John Stuart Mill in his work *On Liberty*. When examining controversial issues it may be helpful to reflect on this suggestion:

> The only way in which a human being can make some approach to knowing the whole of a subject, is by hearing what can be said about it by persons of every variety of opinion, and studying all modes in which it can be looked at by every character of mind. No wise man ever acquired his wisdom in any mode but this.

Analyzing Sources of Information

The Opposing Viewpoints books include diverse materials taken from magazines, journals, books, and newspapers, as well as statements and position papers from a wide range of individuals, organizations and governments. This broad spectrum of sources helps to develop patterns of thinking which are open to the consideration of a variety of opinions.

Pitfalls to Avoid

A pitfall to avoid in considering opposing points of view is that of regarding one's own opinion as being common sense and the most rational stance and the point of view of others as being only opinion and naturally wrong. It may be that another's opinion is correct and one's own is in error.

Another pitfall to avoid is that of closing one's mind to the opinions of those with whom one disagrees. The best way to approach a dialogue is to make one's primary purpose that of understanding the mind and arguments of the other person and not that of enlightening him or her with one's own solutions. More can be learned by listening than speaking.

It is my hope that after reading this book the reader will have a deeper understanding of the issues debated and will appreciate the complexity of even seemingly simple issues on which good and honest people disagree. This awareness is particularly important in a democratic society such as ours where people enter into public debate to determine the common good. Those with whom one disagrees should not necessarily be regarded as enemies, but perhaps simply as people who suggest different paths to a common goal.

Developing Basic Reading and Thinking Skills

In this book carefully edited opposing viewpoints are purposely placed back to back to create a running debate; each viewpoint is preceded by a short quotation that best expresses the author's main argument. This format instantly plunges the reader into the midst of a controversial issue and greatly aids that reader in mastering the basic skill of recognizing an author's point of view.

A number of basic skills for critical thinking are practiced in the activities that appear throughout the books in the series. Some of the skills are:

Evaluating Sources of Information   The ability to choose from among alternative sources the most reliable and accurate source in relation to a given subject.

Separating Fact from Opinion   The ability to make the basic distinction between factual statements (those that can be demonstrated or verified empirically) and statements of opinion (those that are beliefs or attitudes that cannot be proved).

Identifying Stereotypes   The ability to identify oversimplified, exaggerated descriptions (favorable or unfavorable) about people and insulting statements about racial, religious or national groups, based upon misinformation or lack of information.

Recognizing Ethnocentrism   The ability to recognize attitudes or opinions that express the view that one's own race, culture, or group is inherently superior, or those attitudes that judge another culture or group in terms of one's own.

It is important to consider opposing viewpoints and equally important to be able to critically analyze those viewpoints. The activities in this book are designed to help the reader master these thinking skills. Statements are taken from the book's viewpoints and the reader is asked to analyze them. This technique aids the reader in developing skills that not only can be applied to the viewpoints in this book, but also to situations where opinionated spokespersons comment on controversial issues. Although the activities are helpful to the solitary reader, they are most useful when the reader can benefit from the interaction of group discussion.

Using this book and others in the series should help readers develop basic reading and thinking skills. These skills should improve the readers' ability to understand what they read. Readers should be better able to separate fact from opinion, substance from rhetoric and become better consumers of information in our media-centered culture.

This volume of the Opposing Viewpoints books does not advocate a particular point of view. Quite the contrary! The very nature of the book leaves it to the reader to formulate the opinions he or she finds most suitable. My purpose as publisher is to see that this is made possible by offering a wide range of viewpoints which are fairly presented.

David L. Bender
Publisher

Preface to
First Edition

In November, 1847, the Communist League, an international association of workers, met in London. The purpose of the meeting was to draft a theoretical and practical program which could serve as a basis for uniting the working classes of Europe. The League contacted Karl Marx, a German philosopher living in Brussels, and asked him to formulate such a program. Collaborating with his close friend, Friedrich Engels, Marx set out to compose a statement of principles which hopefully would satisfy the needs of the League. He achieved much more than that immediate goal. What he produced was *The Manifesto of the Communist Party*, a work which has succeeded in becoming the guiding credo or "bible" of the international Communist movement.

When Marx composed the *Manifesto*, he was not what would be referred to today as a communist. Essentially, he was a socialist and like virtually all socialists of his day, he was an avowed enemy of capitalism. An economic system, capitalism had begun flourishing throughout Western Europe in the eighteenth and early nineteenth centuries. Its positive achievements included an unprecedented increase in the quality and quantity of goods and services available for public consumption. The introduction of the factory system and the absence of governmental regulations or restrictions in the affairs of business (i.e. free enterprise) were largely responsible for this increase. However its negative aspects were equally unprecedented and significant. The tremendous growth in business and its accompanying profits were being generated by a hapless and ever-increasing labor force. Men, women, and children were required to work fourteen to eighteen hour days for wages barely consistent with economic survival. Moreover, working conditions were as miserable as wages, since factories, mines, and their like were characteristically overcrowded and often unsafe.

Marx theorized that capitalism was not fated to last indefinitely. In the near future, the workers of the world would react to their oppressive situation by revolting against their capitalist exploiters. Marx believed that once the revolution was complete and the final vestiges of capitalism were eliminated, human society would become a workers' paradise in which all would labor according to their abilities and receive according to their needs.* It was his task, and the task of all socialist intellectuals, to raise the

---

*This theory of Marx held that all history passed through several stages. Communism, or that stage in which there would be worldwide economic equality, was to be the final stage.

revolutionary consciousness of the masses of the world.

However, the revolution which Marx anticipated in his lifetime never came. One of the primary reasons for this was that the laboring classes began experiencing a gradual improvement in their economic and political lives. By the last quarter of the nineteenth century, the governments of the industrialized democracies of Western Europe and America began passing laws aimed at bettering the working conditions and wages of workers. Moreover, there was a slow yet steady broadening of the voting franchise.

At this point, as more and more workers obtained the right to vote, a significant split occurred within the socialist movement. While both sides in this split rigidly held to the belief that capitalism must be replaced by socialism, they differed, often with savagery, as to how the change should take place. One group remained unimpressed by the governmental intervention on behalf of the workers and adhered to Marx's concept of revolution. The other group began advocating gradualism, that is socialism by parliamentary means. Simply put, the socialist controversy was reduced to this single question: Should capitalism be eliminated by blood or by votes?

About this time (i.e. when socialism divided into two camps) communism began coming into its own as a movement apart from socialism. Originally, the Communists were a small extremist group of revolutionaries within the European socialist movement. The Communist party in Russia was one such group. Under the leadership of Nikolai Lenin, the Russian Communists gained control of that country's government following a successful revolution in 1917. And it was after the Russian revolution that socialism and communism began their final parting of the ways.

The crux of the controversy between socialism and communism centers upon the doctrines of Karl Marx, or, more specifically, the question of which of the two movements is truly Marxist. Socialists disavow all connections, theoretical and otherwise, with communism. They claim that the Soviet Union, and other Communist states, are totalitarian prostitutions of Marxian socialism. The following, adopted at the Socialist International Conference held in Germany in 1951, encapsulates the socialist attitude toward communism:

> Communism falsely claims a share in the socialist tradition. In fact it has distorted that tradition beyond recognition. It has built up a rigid theology which is incompatible with the critical spirit of Marxism.
>
> International communism is the instrument of a new imperialist state. Wherever it has achieved power it has destroyed freedom or the chance of gaining freedom. It is based on a militarist bureaucracy and a terrorist police. By producing glaring contrasts of wealth and privilege it has created a new class

society. Forced labor plays an important part in its economic organization.

Most communists, of course, deny these charges. Thus it is the purpose of this book to examine life under communism utilizing the above statement drafted by the Socialist International as a frame of reference. Additionally, the relationship between the communist and capitalist worlds will be considered. The viewpoints concentrate upon the Soviet Union since militarily it is the most powerful, and politically and economically it is the most successful contemporary communist state. For the most part, the viewpoints avoid theoretical debates, focusing instead upon the more practical issues of freedom versus tyranny and peaceful coexistence versus war.

Preface to Second Edition

It is with pleasure and an enormous degree of satisfaction that the second edition of Greenhaven Press's *ISMS Series: Opposing Viewpoints* has been published. The Series was so well received when it initially was made available in 1978 that plans for its revision were almost immediately formulated. During the following years, the enthusiasm of librarians and classroom teachers provided the editor with the necessary encouragement to complete the project.

While the Opposing Viewpoints format of the series has remained the same, each of the books has undergone a major revision. Because the series is developed along historical lines, materials were added or deleted in the opening chapters only where historical interpretations have changed or new sources were uncovered. The final chapters of each book have been comprehensively recast to reflect changes in the national and international situations since the original titles were published.

The Series began with six titles: *Capitalism, Communism, Internationalism, Nationalism, Racism,* and *Socialism.* A new and long overdue title, *Feminism,* has been added and several additional ones are being considered for the future. The editor offers his deepest gratitude to the dedicated and talented editorial staff of Greenhaven Press for its countless and invaluable contributions. A special thanks goes to Bonnie Szumski, whose gentle encouragement and indomitable aplomb helped carry the developing manuscripts over many inevitable obstacles. Finally, the editor thanks all future readers and hopes that the 1986 edition of the *ISMS Series* will enjoy the same reception as its predecessor.

"The Great Debate": Communism, Socialism, or Capitalism?

Introduction

Jeremy Bentham (1748-1832), the British philosopher, wrote that "it is the greatest good to the greatest number which is the measure of right and wrong." While Bentham's dictum ignores the possibility of absolute measures of right and wrong, it does have a practical appeal. Undoubtedly, most people do tend to measure the worth of things according to the amount of good or bad which they produce.

Since the French Revolution (1789), political and economic systems have generally been judged by a similar yardstick. If the systems are such that they offer freedom, security, and plenty to a majority of citizens thay are deemed good and receive wide support. If they do not provide these things, they are considered bad.

In the "Great Debate" between communism, capitalism and socialism, supporters of each doctrine borrow a page from Bentham, claiming that their respective philosophies offer the greatest good to the greatest number. Capitalism is held to deliver the widest latitude for individual freedom by minimizing the role of government in the business affairs of a nation. Communists maintain that the greatest freedom, freedom from want, can only be realized when the abuses of big business are eliminated. They claim that a free market, characteristic under capitalism, has led to the exploitation of the poor (or many) by the rich (or few). Socialism, while ideologically close to communism, is said to be beneficial to the masses without resorting to the excesses inherent in both capitalism and communism.

The following viewpoints are excerpts from a debate which took place at Mecca Temple in New York City on February 2, 1930. Presented under the auspices of the League for Public Discussion, Edwin R.A. Seligman, Fenner Brockway, and Scott Nearing defended capitalism, socialism, and communism respectively. The subject debated was: Resolved: That capitalism offers more to the workers of the world than socialism or communism. Although over half a century has elapsed since the debate, it is significant that the arguments offered by the debaters have lost little relevance.

20

"The first achievement of Capitalism...is the amount of wealth that is produced under our present system."

The Virtues of Capitalism

Edwin R.A. Seligman

Professor Edwin R.A. Seligman of Columbia University was the first debater to speak. After defining capitalism, socialism, and communism, he proceeded to defend capitalism. Mr. Seligman based his defense upon what he considered to be capitalism's three great achievements: "The production of wealth in unheard of quantity, the development of opportunity in a way that has never been known, the development of liberty—slow, gradual, but still also in a way that has hitherto been utterly unknown."

As you read, consider the following questions:

1. How does Mr. Seligman's definition of capitalism compare to his definitions of socialism and communism.
2. Why does he believe that capitalism is superior to socialism and communism?

E.R.A. Seligman, in *Capitalism, Socialism, Communism* by The League for Public Discussion, February 2, 1930.

Capitalism [is] an economic system which acknowledges the rights of private property and which puts into the hands of one social class the whole machinery of production, from the acquisition of the raw material up to the disposition of the final product.

By Socialism I mean that economic system which, while acknowledging private property in consumption, takes private property in production out of the hands of the individual and which, therefore, puts into the hands of the government or its accredited representatives the entire process of production from beginning to end.

And by Communism I understand an economic system which goes one step further, which abolishes private property altogether, whether in production or in consumption, and which does away with the other accompaniments of private property which are accepted by Socialism, such as the family and all the other results of the bourgeois system....

Widened Production

Now, then, the first of the points that I want to make is to call attention to the achievements of Capitalism. What has Capitalism done for the world and what does it promise for the future? I should put its achievements under three heads. First and foremost, it has brought about an amplitude or a wealth of production which has never before been known....And the circle of the comfort-receiving class under Capitalism is continually expanding instead of restricting. The first achievement of Capitalism, therefore, is the amount of wealth that is produced under our present system.

Opportunity and Freedom

In the second place, I should put the opportunities opened to the world and to the individual—opportunities which have never existed before. The world has always been so constituted, and probably will always be so constituted, that some people will have a better chance, will have a better likelihood of availing themselves of their opportunities. But, under previous economic systems, those opportunities were not available. The immense progress which we must ascribe to Capitalism is that the number of people to whom these opportunities are vouchsafed is continually growing, expanding from the privileged class of a very small scope to a greater and continually greater circle of people who may avail themselves of these privileges.

In the third place, under the modern system of Capitalism, which means the domination of competition, there has grown an amount of freedom which has never before been known in the history of the world. Freedom is indeed a relative thing. But, after all, the freedom to own one's self as against slavery, the freedom to express one's opinion, the freedom to achieve one's own soul—those things, while by no means 100 per cent under out present system, have been attained to a very much greater extent than in any other system that has ever been known in the world.

Thus, ladies and gentlemen, you have these three great achievements: The production of wealth in unheard of quantity, the development of opportunity in a way that has never been known, the development of liberty—slow, gradual, but still also in a way that has hitherto been utterly unknown....

Why Capitalism?

Why do I stand for Capitalism? Because, so far as Socialism is concerned, it falls down completely on the first point to which I referred. Under Socialism you will not get, and do not get in any of the manifestations which we have of it, as much production as you have under Capitalism.

Every form of government activity is to a certain extent Socialism. Public education is Socialism. The Post Office is Socialism. The street cars in San Francisco are Socialism. But so also in this country, we have had a few examples of a more developed Socialism, as the gas supply in Philadelphia, or the railway system here during the war, or the government merchant marine—all these show us conclusively that in a community, at all events, like that of the United States, the waste, the inefficiency, the corruption, the lack of individual ambition all result in such a diminution of production that, instead of surplus, you have deficit and, instead of prosperity, you have poverty.

Economics and Freedom

Wage and price controls are at the very heart of Socialism. You can't have a totalitarian government without wage and price controls and you can't have a free country with them. Why? You cannot impose slavery upon people who have economic freedom. As long as people have economic freedom, they will be free.

Gary Allen, *None Dare Call It Conspiracy.*

And to come to Communism—if there were time I should like to read this to you. But I haven't time. I can only give you the name of a book by a man who, until recently, was a member of the Community Party—Panait Istrati—which is written in French—a book which in one month went through seventeen editions—and this book, which appeared only a few weeks ago, has gone through eleven editions. That man, who knows his Russia as well as anyone makes his quotations from official Communist sources and from official Communist papers. He gives us a picture of the life of the 158,000,000 out of the 160,000,000 Russians which, to my mind, is the most horrible, the most terrible presentation that has ever

Chicago World's Fair (1893), an achievement of capitalism.
United Press International, Inc.

been given by any human being. The picture that it gives of life, in economic conditions, in moral conditions, in educational conditions, is such as to throw into the discard the very worst things that we see not alone in our Capitalism of today, as down South or in the coal mines or on the fields of this vast country, but the very worst manifestations of Capitalism in its beginnings, in England or on the continent.

I would ask all of you who have any doubts as to what is better for the average man to read some of these devastating pages of "Naked Russia," by Panait Istrati.

What Capitalism Has Done

But the time is almost up, and I want to devote the last two or three minutes to my chief point, which is this: that Capitalism carries within itself the seeds of possibilities which are absent in both of the others. Capitalism is developing in this country two things which have never existed before. The one is a system of social regulation whereby, through government, through society, a system is gradually being evolved which, while preserving competition, raises its level. And secondly, Capitalism is developing, especially among our foremost captains of industry, a sense of social responsibility which never existed before under any other system. It is a system which, under men like Ford, under men like Owen D. Young, under men like any of our great captains of industry, recognizes the doctrine that has been taught by economists for years, the doctrine of the economy of high wages, the doctrine that a workman should at least be treated as well as the machine, the doctrine that there is such a thing as a social responsibility of the Capitalist....

Take Communism as It Is

Don't be deluded by promises. Don't think of Communism with its five-year program, which will never be realized. Take Communism as it is. Take Communism with the difference between the ideology of the enthusiast and the actual facts of the present.

As regards Socialism, while we have never yet had a chance to see what Socialism means in practice, anyone knows what practical Socialism means in this country when, for instance, under the Philadelphia gas regime, we had poor gas, with its deficit and corruption, and when the enterprise was turned over to a private company we got, as at present, good gas and cheaper gas and a large profit which even now goes to decrease the taxes of the community.

So that, ladies and gentlemen, I close this presentation by saying that Capitalism, substantively and actually, gives us what the others have not yet given us and that it promises us far more than either of our adversaries, I think, can really, with justice, promise.

"The Socialist method is a constructive method."

The Virtues of Socialism

Fenner Brockway

Fenner Brockway, defending socialism, was the next speaker. A member of the British Parliament and political secretary of the Independent Labor party, he had served several prison sentences during World War I for his socialist beliefs. Mr. Brockway's criticism of capitalism was moralistic in tone and content. Agreeing with Mr. Seligman that capitalism has produced material riches, the problem, he contended, is "how mankind can become their [i.e. material riches] master instead of being their slave, as it is today." He attacked communism because it advocates revolutionary violence which, he maintained, would inevitably lead to dictatorship.

As you read, consider the following questions:

1. How does Mr. Brockway defend socialism against Mr. Seligman's argument that capitalism allows the widest latitude for human freedom?
2. Why does the author believe that socialism is superior to capitalism and communism?

Fenner Brockway, in *Capitalism, Socialism, Communism* by The League for Public Discussion, February 2, 1930.

As one of the participants in the debate, I [will] comment upon the definitions of Professor Seligman. Very largely, I accept them. I accept his definition that Capitalism means that the whole machinery of production is in the hands of one social class. I accept his definition that Socialism means that the machinery of production is in the hands of the community, whilst private property in personal belongings remains. My one doubt is his definition of Communism, as to whether, under Communism, private property in personal belongings would be entirely abolished. I don't think that even my friend, Scott Nearing, would suggest that this audience of six thousand should own one toothbrush for its communal use....

The problem which we are really discussing tonight is how, under modern conditions, the greatest possibilities of a full, a free, a just and a human life can be secured. I would reply to Professor Seligman, when he says that Capitalism is still a child, by saying that the human race is still only a child. The human race is struggling so that its mental and moral and spiritual qualities may become master of the material forces in the universe. We already realize the marvelous latent possibilities that there are in manhood, the marvelous possibilities of seeking for truth and seeking for beauty and expressing truth and expressing beauty. But yet I think we must all realize that, under our Capitalist civilization, we are also much the slave to material things, material things are so much our masters, that our real humanity hasn't yet been released from its imprisonment, the real qualities of mind and of spirit have not been released.

A Moral Problem

Your business classes today engaged in the struggle for making fortunes, molding their mind in that material fashion—they are not human beings; they are monetary registers. Their minds and their spirits haven't begun to grow to a full human life. Your working classes today engaged in the struggle for existence, going into the factory with the tension of the modern mechanical inventions, always having before them the fear of being fired—that struggle to make ends meet again imprisons in them all that is finer, all that is better, all that is really human in their nature. And even the professional classes, the classes which are able at the universities to try to discover truth, the medical man anxious to express his science, the professor engaged in his reserach—even that professional class is largely imprisoned today, because that professional class is dependent upon those who have wealth in the community; and too often that material power of wealth crushes even the search for truth and the use for truth which is within your professional class.

So I say to my friend, Professor Seligman, that our problem today is not the problem of material production. That problem has been solved. The problem today is with material riches vast in our community, how mankind can become their master instead of being their slave, as it is today....

What Is Freedom?

First, therefore, Socialism is an indictment of Capitalism because Capitalism does not use its material wealth and because its method of distribution of its wealth is unjust.

Secondly, our indictment of Capitalism is that it does not allow the human freedom of which Professor Seligman spoke. I should have loved to have followed him into his argument that freedom of speech is allowed in the Capitalist world. But I want to tell him, and I want to tell all of those middle-class people who seem to regard the freedom of speech as the end-all of human liberty, that the real liberty is the liberty to live, the real liberty is liberty to work and liberty to receive enough from the work to live a full human life....

Capitalism Is Useless

Having outlived its social usefulness, capitalism must give way to a new social order—a social order wherein government shall rest on industry, on the basis of useful occupations, instead of resting on territorial (political) representation. This new system can only be the Socialist form of government if the needs of the vast majority are to be served and if progress is to be the law of the future as it has been in the past.

Socialist Labor party, *Declaration of Fundamental Principles.*

My friends, freedom means that the workers in the workshops, in industry, must not merely be wage-slaves who go into the workshop to do their job and get a wage. Industrial freedom means that the workers must have a share in the ownership of their industry, must have a share in the control of the conditions of their industry, must be able to have a voice in the determination of their conditions; so that when they enter their factory or their workshop, they are not going to get a wage in return for labor and the profits to go to the owner, but they are there to enter the workshop or the factory to render service to the community, knowing that they and their fellow workers shall determine the conditions of their life and the conditions of their living. That is what industrial democracy means. That is what Socialism means....

Superiority of Socialism

But the last point to which I come is the point of difference between my friend, Scott Nearing, and myself; and that point of difference is not so much regarding the goal as the transition from

Capitalism to the goal. The Communist method is based on the belief that that change can only take place inevitably by clash and by violence and, therefore, it desires to prepare the working class to take part in that conflict. When that clash and violence has occurred, then a dictatorship must be assumed, and under that dictatorship inevitably there will be hard and cruel persecution....

Socialism Is Constructive

The Socialist method is a constructive method. It believes that you can construct Socialism by changing public opinion, by building up your industrial organizations, by building up your political organizations, by capturing the machinery of the state. It would bring abut the transition from Capitalism to Socialism, from within by control of industrial organization, and from above by control of the political state....I belong to that group of Socialists which believes that if we can create the human will for Socialism, if we can develop the constructive capacity for Socialism, then if we will have the courage to accept the opportunity when it comes, those of us of this generation, and lay the foundation of this new social order, we will enable those who follow us to build it in all its truth and in all its beauty.

"[Communism] means the suppression and elimination of...class privilege and every other vestige of this present system of economic exploitation."

The Virtues of Communism

Scott Nearing

The final speaker, defending communism, was Scott Nearing. Ironically, he recently had been expelled from the Communist party of the United States because of a heated dispute with the Party leadership over doctrinal matters. His expulsion, however, did not diminish his ardor for communism. Mr. Nearing's attack on capitalism centered upon what he believed is its exploitative and militaristic nature. It is the "masses" of the world, he asserted, who must "organize" if capitalism, a "declining, disintegrating, dying, rotting system," is to be replaced by communism.

As you read, consider the following questions:

1. What does the author mean when he says that Mr. Brockway and the socialists of the Second International had become "adjuncts of economy and the political state"?
2. Why does the author believe that communism is superior to capitalism and socialism?

Scott Nearing, in *Capitalism, Socialism, Communism* by The League for Public Discussion, February 2, 1930.

The issue before us is not an issue of definitions. I should like to paraphrase Mr. Brockway's statement of the issue in this form: How can we organize the world so that the masses of human beings shall enjoy the fullest possibilities for life? I wish, in my first speech, to give the Communist answer to that question....

Communism says to the masses of the workers, "You cannot afford to accept collaboration with the Capitalist class in any form. Where you collaborate you defend, you assist, you protect, you promote these very interests."...

Capitalist Exploitation

Communism holds that the idea of the national economy and the nation-state are already historically outworn. They have performed their functions, as Professor Seligman points out. But that function is a completed, or nearly completed, function. And the question now is, as I said a few moments ago, how can we organize the modern world so that the masses of people shall enjoy the greatest possibilities of life?

Communism looks upon the national economy and the nation-state as a part of Capitalist organization, a system of exploitation built upon class privilege, preserving poverty as a basis for low labor costs, a system extending its area of exploitation through conquest and colonization over the whole non-Capitalist world, a system building a vast military machine that constitutes the largest single item of expense in the budget of every single modern Capitalist state, a system periodically engaged, one nation-state against another nation-state, in destroying its rivals and competitors through the prosecution of war.

This is the system of Capitalist economy and power—exploitation, poverty, colonialism, militarism, war. This is not the system which Professor Seligman described to you....

I said that this was not a question of definitions but a question of how we shall organize the world, and I propose not to define Communism but to try to give you, in the time that I have at my disposal in this first speech, the answer that the Communists make to the question, "How shall we organize the world that the masses may have the largest possibility for full and complete living?"

Workers Must Organize

First of all, as my immediate predecessor has said, "Communists say to the working masses, 'Organize! Take over the economic, political and social machinery. Maintain it during the transition period under the rigid control of the producers.'" This means what is commonly called the dictatorship of the proletariat. It means the suppression and elimination of...class privilege and every other vestige of this present system of economic exploitation and military organization and preparation....

The Communists, therefore, say to the workers "Organize. Take

31

over the economic and political machinery, and maintain it during the transition stage under the rigid dictatorship of the producers. And during that stage lay the foundations of a world for the workers."...

Now, let us go on, because we have only just begun. This is only the first stage. Organize! Set up the control of the working class throughout the world, for what? To do what? To establish a planned economy in place of the chaos which exists in England, in the United States, in Germany, in every other Capitalist state; to build a system of economy according to a scientific plan. Instead of letting every little businessman or every big business trust go his own way or its own way, call together a group of responsible administrators and experts and plan out the economy, just as in the United States and England they plan out political organization. The function of parliament, the function of the Congress of the United States is to plan political life. The function of the state planning commission in Russia is to plan economic life.

Capitalism Is Self-Destructive

Capitalism did not arise because capitalists stole the land or the workmen's tools, but because it was more efficient than feudalism. It will perish because it is not merely less efficient than socialism, but actually self-destructive.

J.B.S. Haldane, *I Believe.*

The Communists say to the masses of the world, "Too long has the control over resources and the control over trade routes and the control over markets and those other economic issues of the world over which the blood of the world is periodically spilled, too long have these issues been solved by a ruthless, chaotic appeal to competition and arms. These issues ought to be solved by groups of intelligent, capable men and women sitting around conference tables and planning the world's economy with the best modern organizational technique which the developed economy of the world today affords."

The Communists maintain that we have reached a stage now in the history of the world when it is possible to organize and plan the world's economy just as it is possible after that, to organize and plan the world's politics....

Benefits of Communism

"Establish a planned economy. Second, abolish exploitation through socialization and production for use." I won't say anything about that, because Fenner Brockway has already covered that adequately. Socialization not of towels and toothbrushes, Professor

Seligman, socialization of railroads, socialization of land, socialization of public utilities...socialization, the control and direction by the workers of the enterprises in which they are jointly and commonly engaged!

"Third, the abolition of poverty by a social guarantee of livelihood." Capitalism guarantees you a street out here with a pavement to walk on. Communism proposes to guarantee to every man and woman and child a minimum livelihood, enough so that no human being ever need again fear individual poverty. If there isn't enough to go around, we will all be hungry. But, if there is enough to go around, let us have it passed around.

Fenner Brockway has also described this point—and this is another point that the Socialists and Communists have in common. Abolish war through the formation of a cooperative world economy and world administrative organization....Abolish war by organizing the economy of the world and building up a world administrative machine on the basis of that economy; in place of the national economy, a world economy; in place of the nation-state, a world-state....

The Communist Message

Here is the Communist program to the masses: Organize. Take over the economy and political machinery. Hold it in the interest of the producers. Don't let the exploiters get their hands on it again. Don't let them interfere. When you have made that step, then begin a planned economy and socialization of production, the guarantee of livelihood, the organization of a world economy and a world administrative organization, and the socialization of leisure and of culture. And on this basis—and, we believe, on this basis only— can the masses of the world gain the fullest opportunities for the expression of life. This means...the rejection of national economy, the rejection of the nation-state, superseding Capitalism in its narrow state-confined political areas by a world system of economic and political and social organization.

Before the masses, the people all over the world, lie two possibilities. Capitalist imperialism, declining, disintegrating, dying, a rotting social system—that is one possibility. The other possibility is a socialized, planned world economy, under working class control, out of which grows the new social order.

The system of Capitalist imperialism, with its twin progeny, poverty and war, stands between the masses of workers and this new social order. The Capitalists cannot change their own system, except in ways profitable to them. The Socialists will not. Militant workers throughout the world must join the ranks of Communism and begin to lay the foundations of that program which I have just tried to describe.

This is the message which Communism brings to the masses all over the world.

Distinguishing Between Fact and Opinion

This activity is designed to help develop the basic reading and thinking skill of distinguishing between fact and opinion. Consider the following statement as an example: "Social, cultural, political, and economic systems differ throughout the world." This statement is a fact with which few people would disagree. But consider a statement which claims that the institutions of one nation are superior to those of another. "The social, cultural, political, and economic systems of the Soviet Union are inferior to those of the United States." Such a statement is clearly an opinion. Most US citizens would probably agree with the statement, but certainly not those who are experiencing disenchantment with life in America.

When investigating controversial issues it is important that one be able to distinguish between statements of fact and statements of opinion. It is also important to recognize that not all statements of fact are true. They may appear to be true, but some are based on inaccurate or false information. For this activity, however, we are concerned with understanding the difference between those statements which appear to be factual and those which appear to be based primarily on opinion.

Most of the following statements are taken from the viewpoints in this chapter. Consider each statement carefully. *Mark O for any statement you believe is an opinion or interpretation of facts. Mark F for any statement you believe is a fact.*

If you are doing this activity as a member of a class or group, compare your answers with those of other class or group members. Be able to defend your answers. You may discover that others will come to different conclusions than you. Listening to the reasons others present for their answers may give you valuable insights in distinguishing between fact and opinion.

If you are reading this book alone, ask others if they agree with your answers. You too will find this interaction very valuable.

O = opinion
F = fact

34

1. There is a Communist conspiracy to take over the world.

2. Communism is the wave of the future.

3. Communism has expanded since World War II.

4. Communism is too idealistic for the real world.

5. The workers in Russia have a great deal of political power.

6. Private enterprise can do most things better than government can.

7. There is more government planning in a communist system than in a capitalist one.

8. There is greater equality under communism than under any other system.

9. It is only natural that workers should prefer communism over capitalism.

10. The capitalist-communist struggle has been responsible for many of the international conflicts in the last thirty years.

11. Workers and owners will always be in conflict with one another.

12. The success of labor unions shows that communism is unnecessary.

13. Capitalism will perish because it is not merely less efficient than socialism, but actually self-destructive.

14. The wealth of all nations is controlled by the few, not the many.

15. The wealth of all nations is controlled by the few at the expense of the many.

16. Wage and price controls are at the very heart of socialism.

17. As long as people have economic freedom, they will be free.

18. Having outlived its social usefulness, capitalism must give way to a new social order.

Bibliography

The following list of books, periodicals, and pamphlets deals with the subject matter of this chapter.

J.A. Andrews — *What Is Communism & Other Anarchist Essays.* Seattle, WA: Left Bank, 1984.

Robert Bideleux — *Communism and Development.* New York: Metheun Inc., 1985.

Leonard J. Cohen — *Communist Systems in Comparative Perspective.* New York: Doubleday, 1974.

Max Eastman — *Reflection on the Failure of Socialism.* Westport, CT: Greenwood, 1982.

Harry B. Ellis — *Ideals and Ideologies: Communism, Socialism and Capitalism.* New York: World, 1968.

James D. Forman — *Communism: From Marx's Manifesto to 20th Century Reality.* New York: Franklin Watts, 1972.

Harvey K. Lehr — *Heyday of American Communism: The Depression Decade.* New York: Basic Books, 1985.

Vladimir I. Lenin — *Declaration of Rights of the Working and Exploited People.* Moscow: Progress Publishers, 1980.

Olga A. Narkiewicz — *Marxism and the Reality of Power.* New York: St. Martin's Press, 1981.

S.P. Novoselov — *Problems of the Communist Movement.* Moscow: Progress Publishers, 1981.

Katharine Savage — *The Story of Marxism and Communism.* New York: Henry Z. Walck, 1968.

Joseph Schumpeter — *Capitalism, Socialism and Democracy.* New York: Harper and Row, 1950.

Hugh Seton-Watson — *From Lenin to Khrushchev: The History of World Communism.* Boulder, CO: Westview, 1985.

Thomas P. Whitney — *The Communist Blueprint for the Future.* New York: Dutton, 1962.

The Communist State: Democratic or Totalitarian?

Introduction

Webster's New Collegiate Dictionary defines democracy as "a government in which the supreme power is vested in the people and exercised by them directly or indirectly through a system of representation usually involving periodically held free elections." Supporters of the communist system in the Soviet Union argue that that nation is a democracy. They point to the Soviet constitution as a thoroughly democratic document. A careful reading of that constitution would compel one to conclude that the Soviet Union is, indeed, a democracy. Power arises from those over whom it is exercised, namely the people. Moreover, a generous system of representation has been provided for and provisions for periodic free elections have been established.

However, a constitution is merely a scrap of paper. No matter how noble and grand are its provisions, it is worthwhile only to the degree which those provisions are practiced. Thus the constitution of the Soviet Union, like *all* constitutions, should be judged by its application, not its contents.

In this chapter, several of the viewpoints exalt the Soviet Constitution for the freedom and self-determination it offers the Soviet people. The reader, however, should remain aware of the discrepancy which often exists between a nation's constitution and its political life. This is not meant to imply that such a discrepancy exists in the USSR. It is merely to warn the reader that conclusions drawn from a single piece of evidence are uncritical and often misleading.

"Terrorism...begins with the abolition of every form of freedom of the Press, and ends in a system of wholesale execution."

Terrorism Is Not Necessary

Karl Kautsky

An Austrian by birth, Karl Kautsky (1854-1938) became a dedicated Marxist while a student at the University of Vienna. However, unlike many Marxists of his day he fell under the influence of Eduard Bernstein, a "revisionist" socialist who preached that a socialist order should be achieved by parliamentary, not revolutionary means. The founder of *Neue Zeit*, a Marxist publication, he was editor of that journal from 1883 until the Bolshevik Revolution of 1917. The violence of the Revolution and the terrorism following it, caused him to increase his verbal and literary opposition to revolutionary socialism and thus alienated him from many leading Marxists. The following viewpoint, excerpted from his 1919 publication, *Terrorism and Communism*, represents one of Mr. Kautsky's strongest attacks against the Bolshevik party and its terrorist tactics.

As you read, consider the following questions:

1. What does the author mean by the following: "Bolshevism has triumphed in Russia, but socialism has suffered a defeat"?
2. Why does the author feel that "European socialism" should take an immediate stand against bolshevism?

Karl Kautsky, *Terrorism and Communism*, London: National Labour Press, 1920.

Many revolutionaries of the West point triumphantly to the fact that Bolshevism* is still in power, and apparently, even at the time when these lines are being written (May, 1919) is still outwardly intact; yet the critics of Bolshevism at the very beginning of its rule prophesied a speedy collapse. This collapse would have actually taken place long ago, if the Bolsheviks had been true to their programme. They have merely kept themselves going by discarding one after another some part of their programme, so that finally they have achieved the very contrary to that which they set out to obtain. For instance, in order to come into power they threw overboard all their democratic principles. In order to keep themselves in power they have had to let their Socialist principles go the way of the democratic. They have maintained themselves as individuals; but they have sacrificed their principles, and have proved themselves to be thorough-going opportunists.

Bolshevism has, up to the present, triumphed in Russia, but Socialism has already suffered a defeat. We have only to look at the form of society which has developed under the Bolshevik regime, and which was bound so to develop, as soon as the Bolshevik method was applied....

A New Class Distinction

Originally they were whole-hearted protagonists of a National Assembly, elected on the strength of a universal and equal vote. But they set this aside, as soon as it stood in their way. They were thorough-going opponents of the death penalty, yet they established a bloody rule. When democracy was being abandoned in the State they became fiery upholders of democracy within the proletariat, but they are repressing this democracy more and more by means of their personal dictatorship. They abolished the piece-work system, and are now reintroducing it. At the beginning of their regime they declared it to be their object to smash the bureaucratic apparatus, which represented the means of power of the old State; but they have introduced in its place a new form of bureaucratic rule. They came into power by dissolving the discipline of the army, and finally the army itself. They have created a new army, severely disciplined. They strove to reduce all classes to the same level, instead of which they have called into being a new class distinction. They have created a class which stands on a lower level than the proletariat....

Soviet Terror

The economic, and with it also the moral, failure of Bolshevik methods is inevitable. It can only be veiled over if it should end in a military collapse. No world revolution, no help from without,

*Bolshevism—Refers to the Bolshevik party, which led the Russian Communist Revolution of October 1917.

could hinder the economic failure of Bolshevik methods. The task of European Socialism, as against Communism, is quite different, namely, to take care that the moral catastrophe resulting from a particular *method* of Socialism shall not lead to the catastrophe of Socialism in general; and, further, to endeavour to make a sharp distinction between these methods and the Marxist method, and bring this distinction to the knowledge of the masses. Any Radical-Socialist Press must ill understand the interests of social revolution, if it really imagines it serves those interests by proclaiming to the masses the identity of Bolshevism and Socialism....

The Price of Success

The Communist theory of the dictatorship assumes that ultimate success in achieving the goal is certain—so certain as to justify a generation at least of poverty, slavery, hatred, spying, forced labor, extinction of independent thought.

Bertrand Russell, *Saturday Review*, 1951.

Among the phenomena for which Bolshevism has been responsible, terrorism, which begins with the abolition of every form of freedom of the Press, and ends in a system of wholesale execution, is certainly the most striking and the most repellent of all. It is that which gave rise to the greatest hatred against the Bolsheviks....

Freedom of the Press

Shooting—that is the Alpha and Omega of Communist government wisdom. Yet does not Lenin himself call upon the "intelligentsia" to help him in the struggle against the rogues and the adventurers? Certainly he does; only he withholds from them the one and only means that can help, namely the *freedom of the Press*. The control exercised by the Press, in every respect free and unimpeded, alone can keep in check those rogues and adventurers who inevitably fasten on to any Government which is unlimited in its powers and uncontrolled. Indeed, often through the very lack of the freedom of the Press these parasites thrive the more.

"Terror can be very efficient against a reactionary class which does not want to leave the scene of operations."

Terrorism Is Necessary

Leon Trotsky

Leon Trotsky (1879-1940) was born in Yanovka, Russia. A socialist revolutionary all of his adult life, he was forced to flee Russia twice (1902 and 1905) in order to escape imprisonment for his anti-Czarist activities. Trotsky was residing in New York City as editor of *The New World*, a Russian journal, when the government of Czar Nicholas II was overthrown. He then returned to Russia and quickly rose to prominence in the Bolshevik government of Nikolai Lenin. Upon Lenin's death, a power struggle surfaced between Trotsky and Joseph Stalin, another Soviet leader. When Stalin managed to gain undisputed leadership of the Soviet Communist party, Trotsky was forced, once again, to go into exile. His continued opposition from abroad to Stalin's regime marked him as an enemy of the Soviet state. In 1940, he was assassinated in his home in a suburb of Mexico City by a man who was believed to be a secret agent of Stalin. Throughout his life, Trotsky was one of the Com-

Leon Trotsky, *Dictatorship Vs. Democracy*, New York: Workers Party of America, 1922.

munist world's leading theorists and most prolific writers. In the following viewpoint from his *Dictatorship Versus Democracy*, Trotsky answered Kautsky's charges by maintaining that terrorism was the most viable method for suppressing counterrevolutionary activity in Russia. (Ironically, the same techniques Trotsky advocated later were directed against his followers whom Stalin alleged were enemies of the Bolshevik Revolution.)

Leon Trotsky praises the victorious Red Army at the Third International in Moscow, 1921.
Wide World Photos

As you read, consider the following questions:

1. By what arguments does the author defend terrorism against Mr. Kautsky's charges?
2. Do you agree or disagree with the author's defense of terrorism? Why?

Kautsky, in spite of all the happenings in the world to-day, completely fails to realize what war is in general, and the civil war in particular....

The problem of revolution, as of war, consists in breaking the will of the foe, forcing him to capitulate and to accept the conditions of the conqueror. The will, of course, is a fact of the physical world, but in contradistinction to a meeting, a dispute, or a congress, the revolution carries out its object by means of the employment of material resources—though to a less degree than war. The bourgeoisie itself conquered power by means of revolts, and consolidated it by the civil war. In the peaceful period, it retains power by means of a system of repression. As long as class society, founded on the most deep-rooted antagonisms, continues to exist, repression remains a necessary means of breaking the will of the opposing side....

The degree of ferocity of the struggle depends on a series of internal and international circumstances. The more ferocious and dangerous is the resistance of the class enemy who have been overthrown, the more inevitably does the system of repression take the form of a system of terror....

The working class, which seized power in battle, had as its object and its duty to establish that power unshakeably, to guarantee its own supremacy beyond question, to destroy its enemies' hankering for a new revolution, and thereby to make sure of carrying out Socialist reforms. Otherwise there would be no point in seizing power.

Fight Fire with Fire

The revolution "logically" does not demand terrorism, just as "logically" it does not demand an armed insurrection. What a profound commonplace! But the revolution does require of the revolutionary class that it should attain its end by all methods at its disposal—if necessary, by an armed rising; if required, by terrorism. A revolutionary class which has conquered power with arms in its hands is bound to, and will, suppress, rifle in hand, all attempts to tear the power out of its hands. Where it has against it a hostile army, it will oppose to it its own army. Where it is confronted with armed conspiracy, attempt at murder, or rising, it will hurl at the heads of its enemies an unsparing penalty. Perhaps Kautsky has invented other methods? Or does he reduce the whole question to the *degree* of repression, and recommend in all circumstances imprisonment instead of execution?

The question of the form of repression, or of its degree, of course, it not one of "principle." It is a question of expediency. In a revolutionary period, the party which has been thrown from power, which does not reconcile itself with the stability of the ruling class, and which proves this by its desperate struggle against the latter, cannot be terrorized by the threat of imprisonment, as it does not believe in its duration. It is just this simple but decisive fact that explains the widespread recourse to shooting in a civil war....

Kautsky Lacks Understanding

Terror can be very efficient against a revolutionary class which does not want to leave the scene of operations. *Intimidation* is a powerful weapon of policy, both internationally and internally. War, like revolution, is founded upon intimidation. A victorious war, generally speaking, destroys only an insignificant part of the conquered army, intimidating the remainder and breaking their will. The revolution works in the same way: it kills individuals, and intimidates thousands. In this sense, the Red Terror is not distinguishable from the armed insurrection, the direct continuation of which it represents. The State terror of a revolutionary class can be condemned "morally" only by a man who, as a principle, rejects (in words) every form of violence whatsoever—consequently, every war and every rising. For this one has to be merely and simply a hypocritical Quaker.

"But, in that case, in what do your tactics differ from the tactics of Tsarism?" we are asked, by the high priests of Liberalism and Kautskianism.

You do not understand this, holy men? We shall explain to you. The terror of Tsarism was directed against the proletariat. The gendarmerie of Tsarism throttled the workers who were fighting for the Socialist order. Our Extraordinary Commissions shoot landlords, capitalists, and generals who are striving to restore the capitalist order. Do you grasp this...distinction? Yes? For us Communists it is quite sufficient.

"Democracy in the U.S.S.R....is democracy for all."

Communism Is Democratic

Joseph Stalin

When Nikolai Lenin died in January 1924, a struggle for control of the government of the USSR broke out among several Bolshevik party leaders. By 1926, Joseph Stalin (1879-1953) had emerged victorious and subsequently deported tens of thousands of the opposition to Siberia. The events of 1926 characterized the domestic policy of Stalin throughout his twenty-seven year rule. By utilizing terrorism—arbitrary arrests, exile, and mass executions—he maintained a fearful and unchallenged dictatorship upon the Soviet Union. When his crimes were exposed three years after his death, he was officially condemned by the new Soviet leadership and pictures, monuments, and other memorabilia of the former dictator were destroyed. The following viewpoint is part of a speech delivered by Stalin at the All-Union Soviet Congress convened in 1936 to discuss and adopt a new Soviet constitution. In it, he explains why he believes that the document is the *"only thoroughly democratic constitution in the world."*

As you read, considering the following question:

1. According to the author, how does democracy in the USSR differ from democracy in capitalist countries?

Joseph Stalin, "International Press Correspondence," a document published November 28, 1936.

There is one group of critics [of the Soviet Constitution who] charge that [it] makes no change in the existing position in the U.S.S.R., that it leaves the dictatorship of the working class intact, does not provide for the freedom of political parties and preserves the present leading position of the Communist Party in the U.S.S.R. At the same time, this group of critics believes that the absence of freedom for parties in the U.S.S.R. is an indication of the violation of fundamental principles of democracy.

I must admit that the....New Constitution really does leave in force the regime of the dictatorship of the working class and also leaves unchanged the present leading position of the Communist Party in the U.S.S.R.

If our venerable critics regard this as a shortcoming of the....Constitution, this can only be regretted. We Bolsheviks, however, consider this as a merit of the....Constitution. As for the freedom of various political parties, we here adhere to somewhat different views. A party is part of a class, its vanguard section. Several parties, and consequently freedom of parties, can only exist in a socie-

Joseph Stalin, dictator of the Soviet Union nearly thirty years.

ty, where there are antagonistic classes whose interests are hostile and irreconcilable, where there are, say, capitalists and workers, landlords and peasants, kulaks and poor peasants, and so on. But in the U.S.S.R. there are no longer such classes as capitalists, landlords, kulaks and so on. There are only two classes in the U.S.S.R., workers and peasants, whose interests are not only not antagonistic, but on the contrary, are amicable. Consequently, in the U.S.S.R. there is no ground for the existence of several parties, nor therefore, for the existence of freedom for such parties.

Only One Party

In the U.S.S.R. there are grounds for only one party, the Communist Party. In the U.S.S.R. only one party can exist, the Communist Party, a party which boldly defends the interests of workers and peasants to the very end. And there can hardly be any doubts about the fact that it defends the interests of these classes not so badly.

Capitalist Democracy

Democracy for an insignificant 1 1inority, democracy for the rich— that is the democracy of capitali,t society. If we look more closely into the mechanism of capitalist democracy...on all sides we see restriction after restriction upon democracy.

Nikolai Lenin, *State and Revolution.*

They talk about democracy, but what is democracy? Democracy in capitalist countries where there are antagonistic classes is, in the last analysis, democracy for the strong, democracy for a propertied minority. Democracy in the U.S.S.R., on the other hand, is democracy for the toilers, is democracy for all. But from this it follows that the principles of democracy are violated, not by the draft of a new Constitution of the U.S.S.R., but by bourgeois constitutions. This is why I think that the Constitution of the U.S.S.R. is the only thoroughly democratic Constitution in the world.

48

"To try and pretend that the Bolshevik Party is truly democratic is to deceive oneself."

Communism Is Authoritarian

Daniel Cohn-Bendit

One of the most frequent charges directed against the Communist party in the Soviet Union is that it is dictatorial. The Party, it is claimed, has degenerated into a closed and rigidly structured bureaucracy which, by its nature, excludes the bulk of the Soviet citizenry from effective participation in government. In the following viewpoint, Daniel Cohn-Bendit, a self-styled anarchist and student revolutionary, attacks the organization and elitism of the Bolshevik party. By dictating from above, he claims, the Party is denying democracy to the masses below.

As you read, consider the following questions:

1. In what way, according to the author, are the Communist and capitalist states alike?
2. Why does the author believe that "democracy cannot exist within the Communist party"?

From *Obsolete Communism: The Left Wing Alternative*, by Daniel and Gabriel Cohn-Bendit, New York: McGraw-Hill, 1968. Used with permission of McGraw-Hill Book Company.

There is no such thing as an isolated revolutionary act. Acts that can transform society take place in association with others, and form part of a general movement that follows its own laws of growth. All revolutionary activity is collective, and hence involves a degree of organization. What we challenge is not the need for this but the need for a revolutionary leadership, the need for a party....

The emergence of bureaucratic tendencies on a world scale, the continuous concentration of capital, and the increasing intervention of the State in economic and social matters, have produced a new managerial class whose fate is no longer bound up with that of the private ownership of the means of production.

It is in the light of this bureaucratization that the Bolshevik Party has been studied. Although its bureaucratic nature is not, of course, its only characteristic, it is true to say that Communists, and also Trotskyists, Maoists and the rest, no less than the capitalist State, all look upon the proletariat as a mass that needs to be directed from above. As a result, democracy degenerates into the ratification at the bottom of decisions taken at the top, and the class struggle is forgotten while the leaders jockey for power within the political hierarchy.

The objections to Bolshevism are not so much moral as sociological; what we attack is not the evil conduct of some of its leaders but an organizational set-up that has become its one and only justification.

Agent of the People

The most forceful champion of a revolutionary party was Lenin, who in his *What is to be done?* argued that the proletariat is unable by itself to reach a 'scientific' understanding of society, that it tends to adopt the prevailing, i.e. the bourgeois, ideology.

Hence it was the essential task of the party to rid the workers of this ideology by a process of political education which could only come to them *from without*. Moreover, Lenin tried to show that the party can only overcome the class enemy by turning itself into a professional revolutionary body in which everyone is allocated a fixed task. Certain of its infallibility, a Party appoints itself the natural spokesman and sole defender of the interests of the working class, and as such wields power on their behalf—i.e. acts as a bureaucracy.

We take quite a different view: far from having to teach the masses, the revolutionary's job is to try to understand and express their common aspirations; far from being Lenin's "tribune of the people who uses every manifestation of tyranny and oppression... to explain his Socialist convictions and his Social Democratic demands,'' the real militant must encourage the workers to struggle on their own behalf, and show how their every struggle can be used to drive a wedge into capitalist society. If he does so, the militant acts as an agent of the people and no longer as their leader....

50

Lenin realized full well that the Party is an artificial creation, that it was imposed upon the working class "from without." Moral scruples have been swept aside: the Party is "right" if it can impose its views upon the masses and wrong if it fails to do so. For Lenin, the whole matter ends there. In his *State and Revolution,* Lenin did not even raise the problem of the relationship between the people and the party. Revolutionary power was a matter of fact, based upon people who are prepared to fight for it; the paradox is

---

Bolshevism and Power

The rule of Bolshevism is based on the possession of power. Thus its fate is sealed. While this party and its friends see ultimate goals which are the same as ours, the intoxication of power has secluded them....Fair becomes foul, foul becomes fair!

Alfred Adler, *Bolshevismus.*

---

that the party's programme, endorsed by these people, was precisely: All power to the Soviets! But whatever its programme, in retrospect we can see that the Party, because of its basic conception, is bound to bring in privilege and bureaucracy, and we must wash our hands of all organizations of this sort. To try and pretend that the Bolshevik Party is truly democratic is to deceive oneself, and this, at least, is an error that Lenin himself never committed.

*"The USSR Constitution offers effective
guarantees of the equality of citizens of all
nationalities."*

Communism Promotes Freedom

Mikhail Krutogolov

Mikhail Krutogolov is a Russian attorney and a corresponding
member of the International Academy of Law. The following viewpoint by Krutogolov appeared in the *Daily World*, the newspaper
of the American Communist party. He contends that under the constitution of the USSR, all citizens enjoy economic security and a
maximum degree of civil liberties, including freedom of the press,
religion, and dissent.

As you read, consider the following questions:

1. In what ways does the author believe that the government of
   the Soviet Union upholds political standards established by
   the United Nations?
2. Basing your answer upon personal knowledge and/or other
   viewpoints in this book, do you agree or disagree with the
   author? Why?

Mikhail Krutogolov, "Rights and Freedoms Under the Soviet Constitution," *Daily World*,
December 5, 1975. Reprinted with permission.

December 5 marks the anniversary of the adoption of the present Constitution of the USSR, which gave legislative embodiment to the results of the radical transformations carried out in the Soviet Union after the 1917 Revolution, including the sphere of civil rights and freedoms.

The Constitution stipulates the main principles governing relations between the state and the individual. They embrace both the political freedoms—freedom of speech, of the press, of assembly, including the holding of mass meetings and the right to elect and be elected, and the social rights—to work, to rest and leisure, to free education and medical service, to maintenance in old age and in case of sickness or disability.

It provides for the equality of rights of citizens irrespective of their nationality or race, and accords all rights to women on an equal footing with men in all spheres of government, economic and cultural activity.

The Right to Work

The Soviet Constitution puts the right to work at the top of the list, since this is the most essential right without which all other rights and freedoms are meaningless.

The right to work is guaranteed by a planned economy, which has done away with unemployment.

When, in 1971-72, new labor codes were adopted in the constituent republics, the article on unemployment benefits was excluded, since during the last 40 years no one has applied to state bodies for such benefits.

The Soviet Union is the only big power which has ratified the two international pacts of the United Nations—the covenant on economic, social and cultural rights and the covenant on civil and political rights.

The Soviet Socialist state was the first in the world to grant an eight-hour working day and a paid vacation to its citizens, the first to provide that the working people are not required to contribute to social insurance funds, because the state has taken this task upon itself.

Civil Liberties Guaranteed

The right of Soviet citizens to unite in public organizations—trade unions, cooperative societies, youth organizations, sport and defense organizations, cultural, technical and scientific societies and professional unions—is guaranteed by Article 126 of the Constitution of the USSR.

Freedom of the press finds its expression not only in the fact that the Communist Party, the Soviets, trade unions and other public organizations and professional unions have their own publications. Along with atheistic journals there are journals issued by churchmen of various religions.

53

Freedom of the press finds its expression also in the fact that every citizen can criticize any organization or any official. Another important freedom is freedom of religious worship. The church is separated from the state in the Soviet Union, and religious belief or non-belief is a private matter for all.

The Soviet experience of solving the nationality question can illustrate the UN Charter's stipulations pertaining to the equality of rights of big and small nations and to the need of promoting universal respect for and observance of human rights and basic freedoms for all people without distinction as to race, language or religion.

The Soviet Constitution

The rights and freedoms validated by the Soviet Constitution and ensured by social and economic conditions have become part and parcel of the life of the citizens of the Soviet state.

Mikhail Krutogolov.

The USSR Constitution offers effective guarantees of the equality of citizens of all nationalities of which there are more than 100 in the Soviet Union. Schools are conducted in various areas of the country in approximately 60 languages. Every nation and nationality is ensured the free development of its culture and traditions.

Statehood in the Soviet Union

But the main thing is that all nations in the Soviet Union have acquired statehood. There are 15 constituent republics, 30 autonomous republics, eight autonomous regions, and ten national areas. They have their own organs of power, develop their languages and cultures and all judicial proceedings are carried out in their national languages.

The rights and freedoms validated by the Soviet Constitution and ensured by social and economic conditions have become part and parcel of the life of the citizens of the Soviet state.

"In the Soviet Union there is no justice, no freedom."

Communism Promotes Tyranny

Vladimir Bukovsky

Since leaving his country, Vladimir Bukovsky, an expatriated Russian dissident, has vigorously campaigned for the establishment of human rights within the Soviet Union. He made national and international headlines when invited by President Carter to visit the White House. The following viewpoint is from an address by Mr. Bukovsky before the AFL-CIO executive council. In it, he describes the dismal condition of the Soviet worker and praises the West for its technological achievements and democratic principles.

As you read, consider the following questions:

1. According to the author, what is the economic situation of the Soviet worker?
2. What does the author say about Western technology?

From an address by Vladimir Bukovsky before the AFL-CIO executive council at Bal Harbour, Florida on February 25, 1977. Reprinted with permission.

When I am asked how many political prisoners there are in the Soviet Union, I answer "250 million." And this is no joke, because we live in a country which is surrounded by barbed wire, in which slave labor exists, in which there is no freedom of movement, where the defense of one's rights is considered to be an offense against the criminal-law code.

When the workers in the U.S.S.R. read in Soviet newspapers numerous, detailed dispatches about all the strikes in the West, many of them seriously believe that you must be dying of hunger. In the Soviet Union, only a person directly threatened by starvation would decide on such an extreme act as a strike. The rare, desperate strikes in the Soviet Union do not occur in the demand of better working conditions or a raise in pay—but only when the workers and their families literally have nothing to eat.

A Nation of Prisoners

The Ukrainian worker Ivan Sivak writes as follows:

"I have been living for 30 years already in the Soviet Union—not living, but existing. During those 30 years, little has changed in the life of a worker. I live in poverty and need. My pay is barely enough to cover food. In addition, in the Soviet Union there is no justice, no freedom. There are limitations in all spheres of life. Everywhere a man feels himself a slave."

That is the way millions of Soviet workers think and feel: deprived of the right to vote, terrorized by the punitive organs. But the process of spiritual liberation is taking hold of more and more new layers of people, and already far more than one academician or writer is becoming the public voice expressing the needs of society.

We are present at the beginning of the process which will bring us to freedom: the process of realization on the part of the workers that they have rights and human dignity. The fate of our peoples—and not only in the Soviet Union but in Eastern Europe as well—will not depend on your position, on your solidarity and support. From whom can Soviet working people hope for support if not from their brothers in the West?

We Look to the West

For decades, we have looked with hope at the West, expecting help from the free nations true to their democratic principles. What have we seen? You know better than I that the greatest building projects of Stalin's five-year plans, using in full force the labor of prisoners, were created through the use of Western—above all, American—techniques and technology. Every time that the hopelessly inefficient Soviet economy is in need of resupply and support, Western countries readily come to its support. They come to help—not the people—but the totalitarian regime.

In March, 1970, academician Sakharov and other participants of the civil-rights movement in the U.S.S.R. made a statement to the Soviet Government, pointing out that Soviet backwardness in the field of automation and computerization of industry can only be overcome in an atmosphere of freedom, with free creative experimentation and scientific research. The Western business world answered this warning by increasing deliveries of computers to the Soviet Union.

For me, the fact is symbolic that I was brought out of the Soviet Union in handcuffs of American manufacture, inscribed with the words "Made in U.S.A." Such handcuffs are broadly used in the prisons and camps of the U.S.S.R.

KGB agents install audio-surveillance devices of Western manufacture in the apartments of Soviet defenders of human rights. In Moscow, exhibitions of Western police technology are organized.

Individual Freedom

Any power must be an enemy of mankind which enslaves the individual by terror or force, whether it arises under a Fascist or Communist flag. All that is valuable in human society depends upon the opportunity for development accorded the individual.

Albert Einstein, London, September 15, 1933.

These are only examples, not more than symbols. In the last analysis, any economic aid to the Soviet Union and Eastern European countries which is not conditioned on definite and strictly fulfilled demands serves only to strengthen that prison of people which goes by the eloquent label of "the Socialist camp."

Soviet Resolution

I see that at present not only Western society but also Government officials—above all, President Carter and his Administration—are beginning to take up a firm moral position in regard to violations of human rights in the Soviet Union. I can only welcome this.

But I know that voices are already sounding against this position. Fears are already being expressed that the Soviet leadership will react and is reacting to this firmness with cruelty and repression, and that maybe it is better not to anger the Soviet Union, but to return to the practice of concession and backstage discussion.

And it is true that the Soviet Union is at present doing everything it can to prove that it scorns all Western protests and will not weaken repressions. At this moment, the most important thing is to acquire patience—not lower your guard, not to expect speedy and immediate results.

Distinguishing Bias from Reason

When dealing with highly controversial subjects, many often will allow their feelings to dominate their powers of reason. Thus, one of the most important critical thinking skills is the ability to distinguish between statements based upon emotion and those based upon a rational consideration of the facts.

Most of the following statements are taken from the viewpoints in this chapter. Consider each statement carefully. *Mark R for any statement you believe is based on reason or a rational consideration of the facts. Mark B for any statement you believe is based on bias, prejudice, or emotion. Mark I for any statement you think is impossible to judge.*

If you are doing this activity as a member of a class or group, compare your answers with those of other class or group members. Be able to explain your answers. You may discover that others will come to different conclusions than you. Listening to the reasons others present for their answers may give you valuable insights in distinguishing between bias and reason.

If you are reading this book alone, ask others if they agree with your answers. You will find this interaction very valuable.

R = a statement based upon reason
B = a statement based upon bias
I = a statement impossible to judge

1. The Bolsheviks strove to reduce all classes to the same level, instead of which they have called into being a new class distinction.

2. Shooting—that is the Alpha and Omega of Communist government wisdom.

3. It was impossible to determine before hand that the Communist revolutionaries in Russia would turn into such bloody tyrants.

4. The problem of revolution consists in breaking the will of the foe, forcing him to capitulate and to accept the conditions of the conqueror.

5. Terror can be very efficient against a reactionary class which does not want to leave the scene of operations.

6. The Communist revolution does require of the revolutionary class that it should attain its end by all methods at its disposal—if necessary, by an armed rising.

7. Who can deny that communism is the wave of the future.

8. Communism may succeed as a system of government – or it may not. Only the future can tell.

9. If we look more closely into the mechanism of capitalist democracy, on all sides we see restriction after restriction upon democracy.

10. It is true that a communist state, no less than a capitalist state, both look upon the proletariat as a mass that needs to be directed from above.

11. To try to pretend that the Bolshevik party is truly democratic is to deceive oneself.

12. History will ultimately determine whether or not the Communist revolution truly brought about democratic reform.

13. A careful reading of the Soviet Constitution reveals that it is the most democratic constitution in the world.

14. The rights and freedoms validated by the Soviet Constitution have become part and parcel of the life of the citizens of the Soviet state.

Bibliography

The following list of books, periodicals, and pamphlets deals with the subject matter of this chapter.

Nicholas Berdyaev	*The Origins of Russian Communism.* London: Geoffrey Bles, 1948.
Cyril E. Black and Thomas P. Thorton, eds.	*Communism and Revolution: The Strategic Uses of Political Violence.* Princeton, NJ: 1984.
N.I. Bukharin	*The ABC of Communism.* Glasgow: Socialist Labour Press, 1921.
E.H. Carr	*The Bolshevik Revolution, 1917-1921.* New York: The Macmillian Company, 1951.
Milovan Djilas	*Conversations with Stalin.* New York: Harcourt, Brace, and World, 1962.
Max Eastman	*The Young Trotsky.* New York: State Mutual Books, 1982.
Karl Kautsky	*The Dictatorship of the Proletariat.* Manchester: The National Labour Press, 1924.
David W. Lovell	*From Marx to Lenin: An Evaluation of Marx's Responsibility for Soviet Authoritarianism.* New York: Cambridge University Press, 1984.
John Molyneux	*Leon Trotsky's Theory of Revolution.* New York: St. Martin's Press, 1981.
Brian Pearce	*Military Writings and Speeches of Leon Trotsky.* New York: State Mutual Books, 1982.
Jean-Francois Revel	*The Totalitarian Temptation.* New York: Penguin, 1978.
Joseph Stalin	*The Foundations of Leninism.* Moscow: Foreign Languages Publishing House, 1924.
Donald Treadgold	*Lenin and His Rivals.* New York: Frederick A. Praeger, 1955.
Leon Trotsky	*The History of the Russian Revolution.* New York: Simon and Schuster, 1932.
G.R. Urban	*Stalinism: Its Impact on Russia and the World.* New York: Gower Publishing Company, 1986.

Life in the Soviet Union: Freedom or Tyranny?

Introduction

Karl Marx and other nineteenth-century communists formulated their ideas for what they felt would be a more just society during a period when capitalist industrialization was leaving thousands of people with unfair wages, unsafe working conditions, poor housing, no money for medical care, no retirement benefits, and little room for intellectual freedom. Communism was a response to capitalist abuses during the Industrial Revolution. Twentieth-century communists still argue that communism is a fairer system than capitalism because it provides people with the social services they need—services most capitalist societies do not guarantee their citizens.

The viewpoints in the following chapter reflect this argument. Konstantin Chernenko outlines the Soviet government's priorities, which include providing more services to its people. Michael Parenti argues that life in the Soviet Union has been misrepresented by the capitalist press. The viewpoint by Mikhail Sholokhov and Alexander Chakovsky boast of the high degree of intellectual freedom enjoyed in the Soviet Union.

Those who disagree with this view of communism point to the social problems still present in Soviet society and the government's abuse of its power. David E. Powell and Konstantin Simis represent these points of view. Anatoly Kuznetsov, a Soviet dissident now residing in England, explains why the rigid censorship imposed upon Soviet intellectuals by the government drove him from his homeland.

1

"The ultimate goal of all our work is improving the well-being of the Soviet people."

The USSR Is a Progressive Society

Konstantin Chernenko

Konstantin Chernenko (1911-1985), succeeded Yuri Andropov as premier of the Soviet Union on February 13, 1984. The following viewpoint is excerpted from his acceptance speech, in which he describes how the Communist party has improved people's lives immeasurably. He also speaks glowingly of the USSR's recent past and of its potentially glorious future.

As you read, consider the following questions:

1. What portion of Soviet income does the author claim was directed to social programs?
2. What problems does Mr. Chernenko admit are still unsolved? What does he plan to do about these problems?
3. According to Mr. Chernenko, what is the importance of moral incentives? Does he suggest there is a need for economic incentives?

Konstantin Chernenko, in a speech to the Central Committee of the Communist party, March 2, 1984.

During the past five years, the complexities of international life compelled us to divert considerable resources to the need connected with the consolidation of the country's security. But we did not even think of curtailing social programs since the ultimate goal of all our work is improving the well-being of the Soviet people. And our approach to this task is broad. We want the people not only to be better off materially, but also healthy physically, developed spiritually and active in social life.

Four-fifths of the national income was directed over the past period to the people's well-being. The real incomes of the population increased. The public consumption funds became richer as well. And this is the source from which money is drawn for education, health services, payment of pensions and the upkeep of housing.

Our Food Program, as well as the program of developing the manufacture of the consumer goods and services system currently being drawn up is also directed at raising the people's well-being. Much is being done now to expand the production of popular commodities of good quality. The modernization of light and food industry enterprises has been started. In this area, we are actively cooperating with CMEA [Council for Mutual Economic Assistance] countries.

Permanent Priorities

Among the party's permanent priorities are such vital problems as the construction of housing and child-care centers and the expansion of the network of hospitals and polyclinics. Last year, more than two million apartments were built—more than in any of the past five years. The housing construction target for the current five-year plan period is very high. But there are grounds for believing that it will be met.

We realize, of course, that the housing problem is far from being resolved, and we will look for ways to further improve housing conditions. What this implies is not only construction with state money. It appears that the expansion of cooperative and individual construction should be encouraged more vigorously. As for kindergartens and nurseries, we have succeeded in easing the situation here. Much, however, remains to be done.

In the coming years it is planned to increase the salaries of teachers and other workers engaged in public education. In the future attention will also be given to war veterans and workers with long job histories, large families, newlyweds and to improving the living standards of the Soviet people in general....

Of course, comrades, what has been accomplished is only the beginning of great work. There are still many things, and urgent ones, to be done. We can and we want to move forward faster. We can and should be much more vigorous in solving the problems of intensifying economic development. For it is only on this basis that it is possible to meet more fully the material and intellectual needs of the people.

Working

In brief, speaking about plans for the future, one should never forget one simple truth: In order to live better, it is necessary to work better. In order to advance successfully in implementing our social programs, it is necessary to ensure the stable, dynamic growth of the economy and, above all, its efficiency....

We have succeeded so far in improving economic indicators chiefly through reserves lying, so to say, at hand, on the surface. We started enhancing order, organization and discipline, and this immediately produced a noticeable economic effect. It is necessary to advance further—toward profound qualitative changes in the national economy.

Living Standards

Many people in the West believe a person to be well-off if he has a car. In our country we think living standards are high because all people enjoy extensive services provided free by the state.

There is no denying that material possessions play an important role in life. But we take the view that living standards are by no means determined simply by the material aspects of life. For a person to lead a truly full life, to satisfy his needs and to face the future with confidence it is much more important to have good health, an education, a rich personality, a secure job suiting his inclinations and security in old age. If we are talking about these basic components of human well-being, then these are a reality for Soviet people.

Novosti Press Agency, *USSR: 100 Questions and Answers*, 1983.

Our economy still has a number of sectors where lack of progress is obvious. The available production potential is far from being fully used. The experimental base of mechanical engineering is inexcusably weak. The share of arduous manual and unskilled work in industrial production and construction is being reduced slowly.

It is a must that we ensure a swift and continuous modernization of all branches of the national economy on the basis of the latest achievements in science and technology. This is one of our basic tasks. Without this, society's progress is simply unthinkable.

Leninist Principles

The party also lays keen emphasis upon the issue of starting a large-scale improvement of economic management and restructuring of the economic mechanism. The main guidelines for this work have been defined. They fully accord with the Leninist principle of democratic centralism....

The matter is that today, as never before, successes in the party's guidance of society depend on the consistent observance of the Leninist principle of the unity of ideological, organizational and economic work. Building socialism and perfecting it means not only the construction of modern factories and power plants and making our land, our villages and cities more beautiful. This is a necessary, but far from the only concern of Communists. While transforming the living conditions of people, it is also necessary to do everything possible for their ideological and moral elevation. Obviously, the tasks of perfecting mature socialism cannot be resolved without a great deal of work to spiritually develop people and their socialist education....

Human Factor of Economic Progress

I have been told that industrial robots have started performing some production operations....There will be more of them with time, of course. But even then, I assure you, the importance of what we call the human factor of economic progress will not be lessened. By this we mean the importance of knowledge, the interests and mood of people. For work is done by man and is acclaimed through man. This old truth will never be made obsolete by scientific and technological progress.

In production, the Soviet worker should always be the full-fledged and responsible master. This aim is served by the Law on Work Collectives which was adopted last year. It is aimed at further developing precisely the managerial initiative of the working people.

The educational force of moral incentives is tremendous in the life of every work collective. In our country work is the basis for social recognition, the source of social prestige. The people are justly indignant at shirkers, people who change jobs frequently and drunkards, who try to use the lofty name of the worker as a cover for their own laziness and slipshod behavior, and even demand public respect for themselves. One of the main objectives of educational work is to form and strengthen in society an atmosphere of respectful attitude to work and, at the same time, of intolerance and contempt for all kinds of idleness, sloppiness and irresponsible attitudes.

"Most people in the Soviet Union live out their lives either in a state of 'quiet desperation' or in pursuit of their personal ambitions."

The USSR Is a Troubled Society

David E. Powell

David E. Powell is a lecturer in the Department of Government at Harvard University. In the following viewpoint, he describes his perception of Soviet society and makes a pessimistic prediction of future problems in Russia.

As you read, consider the following questions:

1. What effect does the author believe the falling growth rate in the Soviet Union is expected to have on that society?
2. According to Mr. Powell, how does the Soviet Union deal with poor productivity?
3. In the author's opinion, how is alcoholism affecting the Soviet society?

David E. Powell, "A Troubled Society," from *The Soviet Union Today*, edited by James Cracraft, 1983. Reprinted by permission of THE BULLETIN OF THE ATOMIC SCIENTISTS, a magazine of science and world affairs. Copyright© 1983 by the Educational Foundations for Nuclear Science, Chicago, IL 60637.

Before the ban on information, the principal Soviet statistical handbook revealed that male life expectancy had fallen from 66 to 64, and that infant mortality had increased from 22.9 per 1,000 live births in 1971 to 27.9 in 1974. The continued silence strongly suggests that conditions continue to deteriorate—or at least have not improved.

Other demographic developments are of a more common nature. Thus, the Soviet population, like that of most other advanced industrial societies, has been growing older. The number of persons of pension age (55 and above for women, 60 and above for men) increases with each passing year. On the eve of World War II, approximately 9 percent of the population were eligible for retirement, but by 1959 the proportion had increased to 12 percent. The 1970 census revealed that the figure had risen to 15 percent, and even though the necessary data from the 1979 census have not been published, Soviet experts put the figure at 15.5 percent today. One out of every 15 individuals in 1939 was 60 or older; the proportion today is one of eight.

The "graying" of the Soviet population has important implications for the country's manpower situation. Inasmuch as the process is expected to continue for the next several decades at least, prospects for continued economic development may well be severely threatened. While greater numbers of pensioners will place increased burdens on the planners' resources, lower birth rates will deprive the economy of badly needed workers for industry, construction and agriculture. Young people are waiting longer before marrying, and married couples are deferring still further the decision to have a child. As a rule, those who do have children have fewer than their parents did and this trend will probably continue. In fact, given the dramatic decline in marriage rates and the equally striking increase in divorce rates, it is clear that the population will continue to expand at a slow pace.

Falling Growth Rate

The rate of growth of the Soviet labor force has fallen even more sharply and promises to continue to do so. According to two U.S. government specialists, the rate of expansion during the period of 1970 to 1990 will be only one-third of that which prevailed between 1950 and 1970. Central Intelligence Agency analysts predict that annual increments to the Soviet working age population will average less than 500,000 during the 1980s; the average figure for the most recent Five-Year Plan (1976-1980) was 2,029,000 persons per year.

As recently as 1950, more than one-fourth of the Soviet population was not involved in "social production" or full-time study; today, the figure is a mere 5 percent. In the past, additions to the work force could be secured by recruiting women who were engaged in household work or rural dwellers who devoted their time to farming their private plots, but these "reserves" have essentially disappeared. Further, the relatively small 1960s generation who will be entering the 1980s labor force will be unable to replace the much large 1920s generation who will be leaving it....

But there is widespread agreement that the level of job turnover in the Soviet Union today is not within acceptable limits. Soviet specialists have termed it "harmful" and say that it is "not justified by any objective need." They term it "a barrier to the progress of society," "a disease" and "a social evil which requires opposition on a joint and organized basis." The data they cite clearly indicate that the large numbers of workers quitting their jobs create economic problems for the enterprises they leave, for those they join, and for themselves and their families.

Thus according to Soviet estimates, between 40 and 75 percent of those who change their place of work also change their occupation. Money initially spent for specialized training is therefore wasted, and new funds are required for retraining. Moreover, low morale and high labor turnover contribute to on-the-job injuries, introduce uncertainties into the housing market, cause a deterioration in "the psychological climate of work collectives" and lead to violations of "labor and social discipline." Sample surveys indicate that most violators of labor discipline have held a given job for only a brief time; they also suggest that some 75 to 80 percent of the workers who do not fulfill their production quotas have worked at their jobs for less than a year. One study found that fully 60 per-

---

Privileged Few

The thin slice of Soviet society that has power also has material comforts. The regime is driven by the need to justify the exemption of the privileged few from the dismal life led by the many. The regime derives its legitimacy, such as it is, from the pretense that it is custodian of history's progressive impulse. That is why the Soviet regime is not—cannot be—in the live-and-let-live business.

George F. Will, *St. Paul Pioneer Press and Dispatch*, October 10, 1985.

---

cent of all defective goods produced at a particular enterprise were the work of individuals who had been employed there for less than a year.

Workers Are Powerless

In an effort to curb high rates of turnover, the Soviet authorities have tried to reward more conscientious workers and to punish "slackers" and "rolling stones." In the past decade, however, a number of Soviet sociologists and industrial psychologists have pointed out that the lack of industrial democracy—Soviet workers have virtually no influence over their wages, hours or working conditions—has given rise to feelings of powerlessness. Such feelings in turn present a major barrier to job satisfaction and to raising productivity. The specialists argue that industrial morale will improve only if a more democratic "microclimate" is established at individual enterprises—if, that is, "everybody, regardless of his position, feels that he is significant and necessary." Some have urged that workers be permitted, even encouraged, to acquire a sense of ownership, and have called for their participation in industrial planning and management. Such an approach would involve bringing ordinary workers into the decision-making process in individual shops and factories, thus encouraging personnel at all levels to help eliminate production bottlenecks and to participate in the setting of work norms and wage rates.

Clinging to Power

However laudable these proposals are, and whether or not they could help raise the level of job satisfaction and so increase labor productivity, it is highly unlikely that there will be anything more than cosmetic change in this sphere. Just as Marx observed a century ago that "no ruling class ever voluntarily gives up state power," the State Planning Committee, the Communist Party and the managerial elite are hardly likely to give up their control over the labor force. Furthermore, the Yugoslav experience with workers' councils, as well as the more recent Polish experience with the independent trade union, Solidarity, cannot help but reinforce the determination of Soviet officials to cling tenaciously to their power.

The post-Stalin relaxation of controls on population movement has resulted in large-scale voluntary shifts of people from the countryside to the cities and from one area of the country to another. According to official data, 62 percent of the population now live in urban areas—although the Soviet conception of "urban areas" and "urban-type settlements" entails a much less concentrated pattern of residence than is normal elsewhere. Still, a massive exodus from the villages has undeniably occurred, an exodus that until very recently showed no signs of slowing....

In a classic study of Soviet migrants and potential migrants, T. I. Zaslavskaia found that most respondents pointed to the quality of life in the city as the primary inducement to leave home. In particular, they cited the diversity of the urban environment, better working conditions, more interesting and remunerative jobs, more and better services, and better opportunities to continue their own education or that of their children. Zaslavskaia was bold enough to add that younger men and women not only found farm work uninteresting but also were frustrated because they were not "masters of the land." Yet if the point is well taken, it is difficult to believe that the system of socialized agriculture will soon be abandoned. Collectivization was introduced for *political* rather than economic reasons, and the same factors that mandate Party control over industry ensure that socialized agriculture will persist for the foreseeable future.

The Rural Exodus

The Soviet authorities still view the rural exodus as "a historically legitimate, progressive process," one required by "the objective laws of social development." Yet officials and specialists alike are becoming increasingly uneasy with some of its consequences. There are four major areas of concern.

Tired of Cabbage

The U.S. Census Bureau reports that the death rate from alcohol poisoning in the USSR is 88 times that in America. Drinking is blamed for more than half of all fatal accidents in Russia....

It is easy to see why those trapped behind the Iron Curtain, including the Russians themselves, would be driven to the bottle. There is nothing good to spend their money on; they are bored, cold, frustrated, silenced—and tired to death of cabbage.

Marvin Stone, *Conservative Digest*, February 1984.

• Rural dwellers tend to move to the city from precisely those areas (Siberia and the Urals) which already suffer from manpower shortages, while villagers in areas of surplus manpower (Central Asia, Moldavia and the Caucasus) have been the most reluctant to leave for the cities. Few individuals, whether peasants or urban residents, are anxious to move to the energy-producing areas of Siberia or to the Sino-Soviet border.

• People who reach the city tend to marry later and to have smaller families than those who remain in the village. There has also been a sharp decline in rural birth rates, largely because of the departure of men and women in their twenties and early thirties. In view of the labor shortage, official concern is clearly warranted.

• The enormous influx of rural folk into Soviet cities has led to or exacerbated a wide array of urban problems, ranging from crowded housing, crime and delinquency to emotional disorders and marital instability. Statistics on crime and delinquency in the Soviet Union continue to be a state secret (as they have been since 1927), but increasingly frequent and pointed press coverage of such matters strongly suggests that anti-social behavior among the young is getting out of hand.

Uncontrolled Migration

• Finally, uncontrolled rural out-migration has been found to be "in conflict with the needs of agricultural production." The most competent and promising youngsters abandon the land, leaving the farms to older, less skilled and less productive workers. Soviet studies showing a decrease in the rural population generally have revealed an even sharper drop among those of working age. In fact, most research actually underestimates the disparity between young and old, since persons listed as "able-bodied workers" on some collective farms include women whose husbands work at nearby enterprises. These women remain on the farms to cultivate their private plots for family needs, contributing little to the collective's effort....

Over the past several decades, there has been a dramatic increase in alcohol consumption almost everywhere in the Soviet Union and among almost all population groups. Soviet sources acknowledge that between 1940 and 1980, when the country's population increased by some 36 percent, sales of alcoholic beverages (corrected for price changes) increased almost eightfold. From 1970 to 1980, when the population grew by 9 percent, alcohol sales rose by 77 percent. These figures indicate that current levels of alcohol consumption are more than just a modern version of the traditional Russian "drinking problem." Indeed, according to U.S. economist Vladimir Treml, the Soviet Union now ranks first in the world in consumption of distilled spirits. Treml has found that total *per capita* consumption of all alcoholic beverages has been increasing by 5.6 percent annually over the past 20 years....

Alcohol abuse is particularly widespread among poorly educated and relatively unskilled urban blue-collar workers, although other groups are by no means immune. In recent years, in fact, the incidence of both drinking and problem drinking has risen in all social strata. But what seems to be especially troublesome to the authorities is the growing problem of alcohol abuse among women and teenagers. Scientists, scholars, journalists and public health law enforcement officials have expressed genuine alarm at this phenomenon, arguing that problem drinking poses a grave threat to society and to the economy.

In the Soviet Union today, alcoholism and associated diseases are the third leading cause of death; only cardiovascular diseases and cancer rank higher. In fact, given the close correlation between heavy drinking on the one hand and cardiovascular problems and cancer on the other, many specialists are inclined to place alcoholism first.

Alcoholism and Birth Defects

There is perhaps even more concern about the link between alcoholism and birth defects. The dramatic rise in alcoholism among women—far more rapid than among men—has been accompanied by increasing numbers of miscarriages, premature births, small babies and brain-damaged children. Medical journals and the popular press note that among the offspring of female alcoholics there is a higher incidence of infant mortality, mental retardation and a variety of serious physical defects.

Many other ills are associated with alcohol abuse in the Soviet Union. For example, approximately half of all divorces are attributed to drinking problems: in study after study, drunkenness is cited more than any other factor as a reason for the wife initiating divorce proceedings. Suicide, too, is often linked with alcohol. Soviet researchers have determined that more than half of all men and women who take their own lives are not sober when they do so, and one investigation found that almost half of those who committed or attempted suicide were alcoholics.

The consumption of alcoholic beverages is closely associated with crime and delinquency. Data from the 1920s indicate that 23 to 25 percent of persons convicted of crimes were drunk when they committed the act; today, approximately half—estimates range from 45 to 63 percent—of all crimes are committed by people who are intoxicated. Certain categories of criminal behavior are especially strongly correlated with drunkenness. Some 60 percent of all thefts and more than 80 percent of all robberies are attributed to intoxicated individuals. Figures for crimes against the person conform to this pattern: 74 percent of all premeditated murders, 76 percent of all rapes and more than 90 percent of all acts of "hooliganism" (a highly elastic term which covers behavior ranging from "disturbing the peace" to "assault" and "assault and battery") are the acts of people who were drunk at the time.

It is unclear whether the Soviet authorities can prevent the situation from getting worse. They have raised the price of alcoholic beverages repeatedly; reduced the number of retail liquor outlets; introduced a wide array of criminal and civil penalties; disseminated anti-alcohol propaganda in the mass media, at schools and at workplaces; and have tried in many other ways to curb the people's desire to drink. But none of these measures has been successful, and even some sort of "dry law" would be unlikely to do the job. The existing problem of illicitly manufactured liquor would only grow worse, and in turn lead to public health and law enforcement difficulties that the regime prefers not to face. Besides, the sale of alcoholic beverages is highly remunerative, providing the single largest source of budgetary revenue for the state.

Constant Turmoil

Turmoil has marked Russian and Soviet society since the beginning of the century. Before the Bolshevik coup, most of this turmoil consisted of anomalies—disruptive incidents and episodes that appeared against a backdrop of conservative institutions and processes. By contrast, the Communist Party has deliberately sought since 1917 to engineer a social and economic transformation, and to this end has consciously revolutionized the country.

As the years have gone by, however, and as the regime has consolidated itself, it has been increasingly inclined to pursue conservative rather than radical policies. The authorities reward hard work and obedience, while punishing those who deviate from prescribed norms. Personal values and behaviors are also, in the main, highly conventional. Children go to school, are taught to be respectful toward their elders, and to seek good grades, admission to an institution of higher learning and a comfortable white-collar job. Adults tend to be highly family-oriented, anxious to obtain a better apartment, a new car, a country *dacha* or various other consumer goods that are in short supply.

"Quiet Desperation"

Although the shortage of consumer goods has led to widespread corruption and a flourishing black market, it would seem that most people in the Soviet Union live out their lives either in a state of "quiet desperation" or in pursuit of their personal ambitions. And in this, it would seem, they behave much as do their counterparts in other countries.

"It is the power of the party apparat that has turned the Soviet Union, in the sixty-three years of its existence, into a country eaten away to the very core by corruption."

The Soviet Government Is Repressive

Konstantin Simis

Konstantin Simis and his wife are Soviet dissidents who were granted the right to leave Russia but were obliged to leave virtually all their material possessions behind. Mr. Simis managed to smuggle the manuscript for his book entitled *USSR: The Corrupt Society* and to publish it in the West despite the KGB's threat to punish them and their relatives if the book were to be published. The following viewpoint is excerpted from that book. It tells of the repression that is pervasive in Soviet society.

As you read, consider the following questions:

1. According to the author, where does the true power of the Soviet Union lie?
2. In what way does the author believe that the state is subordinate to the Communist party?
3. How does "power in the hands of a few" contribute to corruption, according to the author?

From *USSR: The Corrupt Society* by Konstantin Simis. © Copyright 1982 by Konstantin S. Simis. Reprinted by permission of the author.

For the reader to understand the place occupied by corruption in the Soviet state and Soviet society, and the way in which the machinery of that corruption functions, he must have at least a general idea about the laws that govern that state and that society and under which its people live. For people born and raised in Western countries that knowledge is not easy to acquire, even for the few who know Russian, read Soviet newspapers, and have an acquaintance with Soviet law. Even they, not having had the experience of living in the Soviet Union as ordinary citizens (perhaps only as diplomats or journalists), find it hard to understand that the newspapers constantly and deliberately paint a distorted picture of events in the country. That is because all the newspapers are in the hands of the single party—the Communist Party of the Soviet Union—which exercises monopoly rule over the country; they are carrying out the propagandistic tasks assigned them by that party.

But for the person who has grown up in a democratic country the most difficult thing to grasp is the fact that ways and means of governing the huge superpower, and the rights and duties of its citizens, are defined not by a constitution or any other written laws but by a whole body of unwritten laws, which, although not published anywhere, are perfectly well known to all Soviet citizens and are obeyed by them.

The present Soviet constitution states that the power belongs to the people, who exercise it through elected soviets—councils—and the government of the country is carried out by the Council of Ministers and other administrative bodies. The fact is, however, that true power in the Soviet Union belongs to the apparat of the Communist party, and it is the members of that apparat who are the true leaders of the country.

Supreme Power

The constitution states that the Supreme Soviet of the USSR is to exercise supreme power in the country: it issues laws and forms and dissolves the government—that is, the Council of Ministers, which is responsible to it. But in real life the Supreme Soviet of the USSR merely rubber-stamps the decisions of the top Communist party organs. The purely decorative Supreme Soviet is necessary to give to the Soviet state a semblance of democracy.

Everything attests to the decorative, propagandistic functions of the Supreme Soviet: it is in session for a mere six days a year, and in the course of its forty-three years of existence there has *never once* been so much as a single vote against a motion submitted by the government, or even an abstention, either in the Supreme Soviet of the USSR or in the supreme soviets of any of the fifteen Union republics that make up the federation that is the USSR. The fictitious nature of the power of the supreme soviets is further borne out by the fact that never in any of these Soviet "parliaments" has any question been raised relating to lack of confidence in the government; no member of the government has even been questioned on any subject....

Here is an example from real life of the subordination of the state to the party apparat, a subordination that now raises no eyebrows. A minister (now retired) who headed one of the industrial ministries for about twenty years told me a story that put it all in a nutshell, both the position in the ruling hierarchy of each of its participants and the subordination of the state apparat to the party apparat.

Totalitarian Repression

We are approaching the end of a bloody century plagued by a terrible political invention—totalitarianism. Optimism comes less easily today, not because democracy is less vigorous but because democracy's enemies have refined their instruments of repression. Yet optimism is in order because, day by day, democracy is proving itself to be a not-at-all fragile flower.

From Stettin on the Baltic to Varna on the Black Sea, the regimes planted by totalitarianism have had more than 30 years to establish their legitimacy. But none—not one regime—has yet been able to risk free elections. Regimes planted by bayonets do not take root....

At the same time, there is a threat posed to human freedom by the enormous power of the modern state. History teaches the danger of government that overreaches; political control takes precedence over free economic growth; secret police, mindless bureaucracy—all combining to stifle individual excellence and personal freedom.

Ronald Reagan, *Vital Speeches of the Day,* July 1, 1982.

My informant had arranged with another minister to transfer to him control of several enterprises. They drafted a proposed Council of Ministers resolution about the transfer and took it for approval, not to the Council of Ministers itself but rather to the department of the party Central Committee apparat that was in charge of their ministries. The department head did not endorse the proposal, and the ministers—one of whom was a member of the Central Committee, unlike the party official—did not even try to dispute his decision or appeal to the Council of Ministers. It is of course possible that they might have succeeded in such an effort with the help of the Chairman of the Council of Ministers, who was a member of the Politburo, but relations with the head of the Central Committee department, on whom they depended, would then have been ruined forever.

Absolute Power

Thus the real power in the Soviet Union is in the hands of the country's only legal political party, whose apparat is not even mentioned in the constitution or the other laws of the land, and whose functionaries are not elected, but appointed by higher party organs. That power encompasses all spheres of public and private life; it is just as absolute on the national level as it is within each district, each region, and each Union Republic.

The party apparat's power is the more nearly complete since it extends beyond administrative matters to the entire economy of the country. All the country's resources—land, water, factories, banks, transport systems, trade and services; educational and scientific establishments; even entertainment—belong to the state, which is to say that they are under the control of the party apparat. That strengthens the party's control over society as a whole and over each citizen individually, since it turns the party into a monopoly employer, able to prevent the employment in any job of anyone who fails to observe the unwritten rules on which the party's power is based.

Governing Daily Life

Not only does the party apparat wield supreme power in the country but it also governs the daily life of the country, from the activities of the Council of Ministers to those of a small factory or collective farm. Each of the nation's districts is administered by the apparat of the District Committee (Raikom) of the Communist party; each region by the apparat of the Regional Committee (Obkom); and each Union Republic by the apparat of the Republic Central Committee. The entire state, finally, is ruled by the apparat of the Central Committee of the Communist Party of the Soviet Union....

The corruption of the Central Committee secretary, living in his government house and provided free of charge from special government stores with all the food he needs to keep his family, and the corruption of the secretary of a remote provincial Raikom, who has none of those legalized perquisites, have a common foundation. That common foundation is power, a power unbridled by the principle of subordination to the law or by a free press or by the voice of public opinion. It is the power of the party apparat that has turned the Soviet Union, in the sixty-three years of its existence, into a country eaten away to the very core by corruption.

"The leadership consciously pursues policies aimed at a more equitable distribution of services, income, and life chances."

The Soviet Government Is Not Repressive

Michael Parenti

Michael Parenti is an author who writes frequently about the Soviet experience of democracy. He wrote *Democracy for the Few* and is a frequent contributor to the *Daily World*, the Communist party's daily newspaper. In the following viewpoint, Mr. Parenti compares the Soviet and American political and economic systems. He seeks to present a "measured evaluation" of Soviet society to the American public.

As you read, consider the following questions:

1. According to Mr. Parenti, what are Communist ideals?
2. What does the author claim has postponed Marxist achievements?
3. In what ways does US society differ from Soviet society, in the author's opinion?

Michael Parenti, "The Soviet 'Powerbrokers'," *Daily World*, August 16, 1983.

The U.S. news media tell us that Soviet leaders are "ruthless powerbrokers" who exercise "power for power's sake." "They are not liberal reformers, but technicians of power" whose "main preoccupation" is "simply to hold on to power." This description of leaders who seek power and position purely for their own sake certainly fits enough U.S. politicians, who pursue office without knowing what they will do once they get elected. Recall how Jimmy Carter waged a brilliant, protracted campaign to get himself into the White House and, once there, evinced only the vaguest notion of what he wanted to accomplish. Yet, the news media assume that in the U.S. the pursuit of office is a natural and proper expression of ambition and public service, and that there are substantive goals beyond power which leaders seek to attain.

Not so in regard to the Soviet Union. The U.S. commercial press seems not to have a thought that Soviet leaders might be motivated by egalitarian and peaceable goals, that they might use power to advance substantive policy rather than use substantive policy merely to accumulate power.

Democratic Rights

In 1982, the Soviet leader Yuri Andropov noted the "social and political significance" of automation for the ordinary worker:

"For as a rule, a man rid of strenuous, arduous manual labor shows greater initiative and more responsible attitude to the task at hand. He gets additional possibilities for study and rest, for participation in social work, in the management of production. He thus can also more fully exercise his political, democratic rights, granted to the working people by the socialist revolution, the rights of full masters of their society, of their state."

To the extent such pronouncements are given any attention in the U.S. media they are treated as nothing more than the official propaganda which the Soviet rulers allegedly feed their people. Soviet leaders, we are told, have long ago abandoned any dedication to Communist ideals, if they ever had any, and now concentrate on power and conquest. Yet, as the sociologist Shirley Cereseto writes, "The evidence demonstrates that socialist countries, with planning geared toward meeting the basic human needs of the entire population and toward decreasing inequality, have made important strides toward such goals in a relatively short period of time even though most began at a very low stage of economic development." Given their professed intentions and actual programs and accomplishments, Soviet leaders and the Soviet system in general certainly seem propelled by a desire to achieve something more than the mindless accumulation of power. Their commitment to the material egalitarian goals of socialism (and Communism) appears to be very much a guiding force, albeit not the only contributing factor in how Soviet policy is formulated.

The U.S. Sovietologist, Samuel Hendel, notes that something

80

other than mere power brokerage and opportunism directs Soviet policy and that the commitment to socialist ideals is more than just an ideological mouthing: property and capital remain socialized; the private profit system is prohibited; social and human services are publicly owned; agriculture remains collectivized; leaders, planners and intellectuals think in terms of scientific materialism; and the leadership consciously pursues policies aimed at a more equitable distribution of services, income, and life chances.

CAPITALIST RECOMMENDATION: Return to the Cold War

Ollie Harrington for the *Daily World*.

The historical experiences of 65 years, including the upheavals of foreign invasion, civil war, the horrendous devastation of World War II, the Cold War and other political crises, have led to an altering or postponement of certain Marxist aspiration. But, Hendel notes, Soviet leaders have been nurtured since birth on Marxism, have advanced in part because of their commitment to that ideology and continue to be influenced by Marxist principles and values. The same may be said of much of the Soviet populace itself. A former Soviet sociologist and pollster, Dr. Vladimir Shliapentokh, who emigrated to the United States, commented in a news conference: "You shouldn't underestimate the devotion of the Soviet population to the dominant values." A U.S. scholar, Wright Miller, observes: "'Building Communism' is one of the most widely used propaganda phrases, and it is a...slogan which seems to inspire a fair number of Soviet citizens."

Communist Motivation

Of course, the U.S. business-owned media do not deny that Soviet leaders and other Communists are motivated by "Marxist doctrine" as long as the doctrine is represented as having nothing to do with humanitarian and egalitarian social practices and can be considered synonymous with a ruthless, mindless and violent quest for power and domination. Thus, as the mainstream press would have it, the Sandinistas in Nicaragua and revolutionaries in El Salvador do not seek power to eliminate hunger, rather they simply hunger for power. In this sense, the press does not hesitate to describe them as dedicated Communists possessed by the supposedly inhuman compulsions of "Marxist ideology."

What is needed, and what we will never get from the U.S. capitalist press, is a measured evaluation of a vast, changing, complex and remarkable Soviet society. The predominance of an anti-Soviet orthodoxy makes a balanced analysis not only difficult but unnecessary (in the minds of our media pundits). Without benefit of extensive inquiry and sometimes without any actual familiarity with the subject being disparaged, the opinion makers "know" and repeatedly make us "know" that the Soviet system is a "failure," and that its leaders are "expansionist powermongers." U.S. journalists and editors may or may not believe it; usually they do. In any case, they get paid for saying so and *are rarely* inclined, or allowed, to say otherwise.

"Anti-communism wants to impose on us its own concept of 'freedom,' although it is interested in only one freedom, the freedom to propagate anti-Sovietism and undermine the socialist system."

Intellectual Freedom Exists in the Soviet Union

Mikhail Sholokhov and Alexander Chakovsky

The following viewpoint by Alexander Chakovsky and Mikhail Sholokhov was taken from an address delivered by each at the 24th Congress of the Communist Party of the Soviet Union. Chakovsky is editor-in-chief of *Literaturnaya Gaseta*, a Soviet literary journal and Sholokhov, a Nobel Laureate, is considered by many to be the Soviet Union's greatest living author. Mr. Chakovsky, Part I, and Mr. Sholokhov, Part II, both express the same view, namely, that Soviet literature must uphold the socialist tradition by supporting the principles of Lenin.

As you read, consider the following questions:

1. What does Mr. Chakovsky see as the greatest danger to literary freedom in the Soviet Union?
2. According to Mr. Sholokhov, what should be the primary aim of Soviet writers?

The 24th Congress of the Communist Party of the Soviet Union, *Voices of Tommorrow*, New York: New World Review Publications, 1971. Reprinted with permission.

I

So-called "intellectual" anti-communism has a carefully worked out strategy and tactic for seeking to influence our writers and artists, to drive a wedge between them and the Party, and demoralize Soviet intellectuals from within.

A current concept which our enemies actively propagate is that of the supposedly inevitable need for every artist to be in opposition to the state. We, of course, can understand the inevitable opposition of an honest and progressive writer or artist to the bourgeois society and state, which rests on violence, falsehood, the power of money and the exploitation of man by man.

Enemy Propaganda

Anti-communism wants to impose on us its own concept of "freedom," although it is interested in only one freedom, the freedom to propagate anti-Sovietism and undermine the socialist system. Who today, comrades, is not championing the freedom of creativity, the freedom of the writers and artist in the socialist world? Among these champions of freedom are the leaders of the CIA, the "Voice of America," the "Voice of Israel," "Radio Free Europe," the BBC, the *London Times, The New York Times*, the South African racists and the Portugese colonialists. Poor things, they can't rest until they win freedom for us! But what sort of freedom can be offered by the capitalist world, which is going through such a profound spiritual crisis? Freedom for violence and cruelty, for racism and pornography, for Zionism and neo-fascism? However, comrades, it was not for this that our fathers and grandfathers made the Great October Revolution, and that we fought against fascism for the freedom and independence of our country. Nor are we building the bright edifice of communism in order to let its foundations be washed away by the polluted torrents of bourgeois propaganda.

Soviet writers are well aware that in the same way that Antaeus drew his strength from his constant bond with his Mother Earth, so they draw their strength, their inner invincibility, from their cohesion and unity around the Party of Lenin, from their unbreakable bond with its great cause.

II

Appraising our literature in depth, we can say with pride that from the days of the establishment of Soviet power, it has served the people honestly and devotedly, and its voice, in the words of our great Russian poet Lermontov—has truly:

> Sounded, like the bell on an ancient tower,
> In the days of both triumph and sorrow of our peoples.

The voice, both in the past and today, has been heard far beyond the borders of our country. Without any false modesty we can

84

say that we have done a great deal in the sense of re-educating people, influencing their spirtual awakening and growth through the medium of art. The militant role in Soviet literature and art in the world process of the development of artistic culture is determined above all by the charge of communist ideology and party spirit that permeates our best works. To put it bluntly, this is what

Soviet writer Mikhail Sholokhov accepting the Nobel Prize for literature in 1965.
United Press International, Inc.

most infuriates our ideological enemies and their accomplices, the revisionists. They would like to persuade us to abandon our clear-cut positions as convinced fighters for socialism and communism, and to renounce party spirit and kinship with the people as the basic principles of artistic creativity.

But it is time for us, too, under the present conditions of unprecedented and increasingly sharp ideological struggle, to go over more decisively to the offensive and oppose the efforts of the renegades and revisionists of all shadings with our unfailing weapon—the never-fading truth of Lenin. This is our paramount task.

The New Generation

Only our Party and the lofty ideals by which it is guided could achieve the fusing together of thousands of creative lives, from Maxim Gorky [an early Bolshevik writer (1868-1936)] down to the healthy young writers of our time, and inspire them to serve the people and their interests....

A talented young generation is now growing up to replace us. The older generation of writers places great hopes in them. We are glad that the relay baton is being passed on to the kind of artists who are needed by our society. These are interesting, patriotically-minded people, probing into the depths of life.

Young people are sometimes cocky and harsh in their appraisals of certain phenomena, but one valuable thing about them is that they are not indifferent. They are inquisitive, forever searching. Sometimes they lack experience. But the future of our literature lies with them, with the young writers. They will create our future, they will be responsible for it. You understand, of course that I am not here dividing our creative youth into the "clean" and the "unclean." I am speaking of young people as a whole. I am speaking about the new writers' reinforcements, the fresh forces of Soviet literature. But let me remind you, we writers of the older generation are also still worth something!

"The best Russian writers were always persecuted, dragged before the courts, murdered or reduced to suicide."

Intellectual Freedom Does Not Exist in the Soviet Union

Anatoly Kuznetsov

Anatoly Kuznetsov is a dissident Soviet author who has resided in England since 1969. A former member of the Communist Party of the Soviet Union and the USSR Union of Writers, Kuznetsov claims he left his native Russia because he could no longer endure the strict censorship facing Soviet writers. In the following viewpoint, he reveals his personal experiences with Soviet censorship and outlines the difficulties and choice facing all Russian writers.

As you read, consider the following questions:

1. How does Mr. Kuznetsov describe artistic freedom in the Soviet Union?
2. What are the three choices which, according to the author, face Russian writers?
3. Using the arguments of Mr. Chakovsky and Mr. Sholokhov in the previous viewpoint, how would you criticize the Kuznetsov viewpoint?

Anatoly Kuznetsov, "I Could No Longer Breathe," *Time*, August 8, 1969. Reprinted with permission.

You will say it's hard to understand. Why should a writer whose books have sold millions of copies, and who is extremely popular and well-off in his own country, suddenly decide not to return to that country, which, moreover, he loves?

The loss of hope: I simply cannot live there any longer. This feeling is something stronger than me. I just can't go on living there. If I were now to find myself again in the Soviet Union, I should go out of my mind. If I were not a writer, I might have been able to bear it. But, since I am a writer, I can't. Writing is the only occupation in the world that seriously appeals to me. When I write, I have the illusion that there is some sort of sense in my life. Not to write is for me roughly the same as for a fish not to swim. I have been writing as long as I can remember. My first work was published twenty-five years ago.

Soviet Repression

In those twenty-five years, not a single one of my works has been printed in the Soviet Union as I wrote it. For political reasons, the Soviet censorship and the editors shorten, distort and violate my works to the point of making them completely unrecognizable. Or they do not permit them to be published at all. So long as I was young, I went on hoping for something. But the appearance of each new work of mine was not a cause for rejoicing but for sorrow. Because my writing appears in such an ugly, false and misshapen form, and I am ashamed to look people in the face. To write a good book in the Soviet Union, this is still the simplest thing to do. The real trouble begins only later, when you try to get it published. For the past ten years, I have been living in a state of constant, unavoidable and irresolvable contradiction. Finally, I have simply given up.

I Could No Longer Breathe

I wrote my last novel, *The Fire*, with no feeling left in my heart, without faith and without hope. I knew in advance for certain that, even if they published it, they would ruthlessly cut everything human out of it, and that at best it would appear as just one more "ideological" pot-boiler. (And that is, incidentally, exactly what happens.)

I came to the point where I could no longer write, no longer sleep, no longer breathe.

A writer is above all an artist who is trying to penetrate into the unknown. He must be honest and objective, and be able to do his creative work in freedom. These are all obvious truths. These are the very things that writers are forbidden in the Soviet Union.

Artistic freedom in the Soviet Union has been reduced to the "freedom" to praise the Soviet system and the Communist Party and to urge people to fight for Communism. The theoretical basis

Anatoly Kuznetsov, Soviet dissident now residing in England.
Wide World Photos

for this is an article that Lenin wrote sixty years ago on ''The Party Organization and Party Literature,'' which laid it down that every writer is a propagandist for the Party. His job is to receive slogans and orders from the Party and make progaganda out of them.

This means that writers in Russia are faced with the following choices:

(a) Simply to go with this idiocy—to let their brains and their consciences have no effect on their actions. If Stalin is on top, then praise Stalin. If they order people to plant maize, then write about maize. If they decide to expose Stalin's cries, then expose Stalin. And when they stop criticizing him, you stop too. There are so very many Soviet "writers" who are just like that.

The Soviet Nightmare

But real life will not forgive a man who violates his conscience. Those writers have all became such cynics and spiritual cripples and their hidden regret for their wasted talent eats away at them to such an extent that their wretched existence cannot be called life but rather a caricature of life. It would probably be difficult to think up a worse punishment for oneself than to have to spend one's whole life trembling, cringing, trying fearfully to get the sense of the latest order and fearing to make the slightest mistake, Oh, God!

(b) To write properly, as their ability and consciences dictate. It is then 100-to-1 that what they write will not be published. It will simply be buried. It may even be the cause of the author's physical destruction. It is a sad thought that Russia has long and deep "traditions" in this connection. The best Russian writers were always persecuted, dragged before the courts, murdered or reduced to suicide.

Soviet Censorship

There is no suggestion, and no recognition of the right of our writers to state publicly their opinions about the moral life of men and of society....Excellent manuscripts by young authors, still completely unknown, are today rejected by editors on the sole ground that they "will not pass" the censor.

Aleksandr Solzhenitsyn, from a letter addressed to the Writers' Union of the USSR.

(c) To try and write honestly "as far as possible." To choose subjects that are not dangerous. To write in allegories. To seek out cracks in the censorship. To circulate your works from hand to hand in manuscript form. To do at least something: a sort of compromise solution. I was one of those who chose this third way. But it didn't work for me. The censor always managed to bring me to my knees. My anxiety to save at least something from what I had written, so that something would reach the reader, meant only that in the end all my published writings were neither genuine literature nor utterly contemptible but something in between.

However much I protested or tried to prove some point, it was like beating my head against a wall. Literature in the Soviet Union is controlled by people who are ignorant, cynical, and themselves very remote from literature. But they are people with excellent knowledge of the latest instructions from the men at the top of the prevailing Party dogmas. I could not force my way through their ranks. Evtushenko managed to achieve a little in this way. Solzhenitsyn managed a little more, but even that is all over now. The cracks were noticed and cemented up. Russian writers go on writing and keep hoping for something. It is a nightmare.

Recognizing Ethnocentrism

Ethnocentrism is the attitude or tendency of people to view their own race, religion, culture, group, or nation as superior to others, and to judge others on that basis. An American, whose custom is to eat with a fork or spoon, would be making an ethnocentric statement when saying, "The Chinese custom of eating with chopsticks is stupid."

Ethnocentrism has promoted much misunderstanding and conflict. It emphasizes cultural and religious differences and the notion that one's national institutions or group customs are superior.

Ethnocentrism limits people's ability to be objective and to learn from others. Education in the truest sense stresses the similarities of the human condition throughout the world and the basic equality and dignity of all people.

Some of the following statements are taken from the viewpoints in this book. Others have other sources. Consider each statement carefully. *Mark E for any statement you think is ethnocentric. Mark N for any statement you think is not ethnocentric. Mark U if you are undecided about any statement.*

If you are doing this activity as a member of a class or group, compare your answers with those of other class or group members. Be able to defend your answers. You may discover that others will come to different conclusions than you. Listening to the reasons others present for their answers may give you valuable insights in recognizing ethnocentric statements.

If you are reading this book alone, ask others if they agree with your answers. You too will find this interaction very valuable.

E = ethnocentric
N = not ethnocentric
U = undecided

1. Russian people are less physically attractive than Americans.

2. Soviet and American male life expectancy are about the same.

3. Russian cities are not as interesting or fun to visit as American cities.

4. The Soviet Union is a country eaten away to the very core by corruption.

5. The Soviet Union now ranks first in the world in consumption of distilled spirits.

6. Russian people are never sober.

7. Americans are nicer than Russians.

8. Problem drinking poses a grave threat to Soviet society and economy.

9. Russian food is more interesting than American food.

10. Unemployment is higher in the United States than it is in the Soviet Union.

11. Young people educated in America don't know how to work as well as young people educated under socialism.

12. The enormous influx of rural folk into Soviet cities has led to a wide array of urban problems.

13. Lenin was much more intelligent than Thomas Jefferson.

14. The American Russian Institute acts as a friendship society between the US and the Soviet Union.

15. Some items available in the US are difficult to obtain in the Soviet Union.

16. Moscow is the most beautiful city in the world.

17. English translators are in great demand in the Soviet Union.

18. Because they are hard to get, drugs are not a problem in the Soviet Union.

Bibliography

The following list of books, periodicals, and pamphlets deals with the subject matter of this chapter.

Ludmilla Alexeyeva	*Soviet Dissent: Contemporary Movements for National, Religious and Human Rights.* Middletown, CT: Wesleyan University Press, 1985.
Bill Anderson	"Why Socialism Fails—Why Markets Survive," *The Freeman,* December 1983.
Vladimir Borisov	"Soviet Social Security System," *Soviet Military Review,* July 1983. Available from *Soviet Military Review,* 2 Marshall Biryuzov Street, Moscow, 123298, USSR.
Werner Cieslak	"The Only Real Alternative Is Socialism," *New Times,* July 1985. Available from Imported Publications Inc., 320 W. Ohio St., Chicago, IL 60610.
The Civil Liberties Review	"Worlds Apart: US & Soviet Ideas About Freedom," September/October 1977.
Gus Hall	"You Are a Historic Necessity," *Daily World,* July 2, 1981.
In These Times	"Coming to Terms with Soviet Society," January 9/15, 1985.
Robert W. Lee	"The Nature of Communism," *American Opinion,* November 1983.
Novosti Press Agency	*USSR: 100 Questions and Answers.* Pamphlet available from the Soviet Embassy Information Department, 1706 Eighteenth St. NW, Washington, DC 20009. 1983.
Boris Rumer	"Structural Imbalance in the Soviet Economy," *Problems of Communism,* July/August 1984.
Fred C. Schwartz	*Why I Am Against Communism.* Pamphlet available from Christian Anti-Communism Crusade, P.O. Box 890, Long Beach, CA 90801.
USA Today	"Opinion, The Debate: Defectors," December 5, 1984.
U.S. News & World Report	"Communism 'Doesn't Fit a Modern Industrial Society,'" February 4, 1984.

Communism and Capitalism: Is Peaceful Coexistence Possible?

Introduction

Ideology plays a large role in foreign policy disputes. While the following chapter ostensibly concentrates on American and Soviet policy toward each other, behind the obvious arguments are the authors' philosophical disagreements. These disagreements take two forms in this chapter. In four of the viewpoints, the authors have contrasting opinions on whether belief in communism is in fact an important motivation behind Soviet policy. John Lewis Gaddis and Marshall D. Shulman believe the Soviet Union is simply behaving like a great power with national interests to promote and protect. US policy could be more effective, these authors argue, if it dropped its obsession with communist ideology and used the classic means of conducting foreign policy, such as the balance of power strategy. Jean-Francois Revel and Richard Pipes, however, believe the West has, to its own detriment, forgotten that communism shapes Soviet policy and its goal is undermining capitalist democracies.

Even though authors Jessica Smith and Aleksandr Solzhenitsyn both consider communist philosophy important to the Soviet state, they disagree over what communism means and how it manifests itself in Soviet behavior. Ms. Smith believes the Soviet Union has consistently worked for peace throughout its communist history. Mr. Solzhenitsyn, however, claims the Soviets continually fight an ideological cold war against the West, which makes violent warfare unnecessary.

"Seeking containment by way of détente succeeded remarkably well."

Peaceful Coexistence Has Been a Successful Policy

John Lewis Gaddis

Many conservatives criticize the policies of peaceful coexistence and détente for being soft on communism. John Lewis Gaddis, the author of the following viewpoint, considers détente, a strategy for peaceful coexistence, a way to contain communism. Dr. Gaddis is a professor of history at Ohio University and has written extensively on containment and US foreign policy. He argues that strategies aimed at peaceful coexistence were not designed to give in to the Soviets, but rather to contain their influence. Furthermore, he believes that such policies have by and large succeeded.

As you read, consider the following questions:

1. What events does Dr. Gaddis use to support his contention that détente, as practiced in the 1970s, worked?
2. Why was détente considered a failure by 1980, according to the author?
3. What are the ultimate objectives of containment?

John Lewis Gaddis, "The Rise, Fall and Future of Détente." Excerpted by permission of FOREIGN AFFAIRS, Winter 1983/84. Copyright 1983 by the Council on Foreign Relations, Inc.

Détente,...was not an end to cold war tensions but rather a temporary relaxation that depended upon the unlikely intersection of unconnected phenomena. There had to be,...approximate parity in the strategic arms race, a downplaying of ideological differences, a mutual willingness to refrain from challenging the interests of rivals, an ability to reward restraint when it occurred and to provide inducements to its further development, and the existence of strong, decisive and intelligent leadership at the top in both Washington and Moscow, capable of overriding all of the obstacles likely to be thrown in the path of détente by garbled communications, sullen bureaucracies, or outraged constituencies. To have found all of these things in place at the same time,...was about as likely as some rare astronomical conjunction of the stars and planets, or perhaps a balanced budget.

As a result, we have tended to see the revival of the cold war as an entirely predictable development rooted in deep and immutable historical forces....

What follows is an attempt to account for the decline of détente not in terms of historical inevitability—because, beyond death, and perhaps unbalanced budgets, nothing really is inevitable in history—but rather as a failure of strategy from which there are certain things we might learn. The emphasis is on deficiencies in American strategy, not because the United States was solely, or even primarily, responsible for the collapse of détente, but because it is the only strategy we are in a position to do anything about. The Russians will have to learn from their own mistakes, which, as recent events once again confirm, have not been inconsiderable....

Détente's Critics

As the concept of détente has fallen into disrepute in recent years, it has become fashionable to call for a return to, or a revival of, containment. The implied message of such groups as the Committee on the Present Danger, and of such members of that organization as have been, since 1981, in positions of official responsibility, has been that we should never have abandoned a strategy that recognized so clearly the nature of the Soviet threat, that provided such decisive programs for action, and that thus served to keep the peace throughout most of the cold war. From the perspective of these observers, the decision to seek détente in the early 1970s was an unwise exercise in wishful thinking, the effect of which was only to shift the signals, in the eyes of Moscow's watchful and ambitious ideologues, from red to yellow to green.

But this assessment reflects a misunderstanding both of containment and of the détente that followed it, for containment never was a consistently applied or universally understood strategy. Like most strategies, it evolved over time and under the pressure of circumstance, to such an extent that its original founder, George F. Kennan, came ultimately to deny paternity when confronted with some of its more exotic manifestations. If one is to undertand where the idea of détente came from and what functions it was intended to serve, one must first be aware of how the idea of containment has evolved over the years....

Détente and Containment

Nixon and Kissinger...embraced "détente" *as a means of updating and reinvigorating containment.* The term had been in use since the early 1960s to connote a relaxation of tensions with the Soviet Union, and although such a relaxation was one part of the new Administration's approach, it would be a considerable oversimplification to say that this was its chief priority. Rather, détente was a means of maintaining the balance of power in a way that would be consistent with available resources. It was a redefinition of interests to accommodate capabilities. It was,...a way to make containment function more efficiently, but through a method at once more ingenious and less risky than the old "massive retaliation" concept.

The Reaction Against Détente

Today an almost predictable reaction has set in—a reaction against what people understand to be "détente." It has set in partly as a consequence of the earlier overselling of this idea; partly because real mistakes have been made here and there, on both sides; partly because an improvement in political relations appeared to threaten the formidable interests vested in a continuing state of high military tension. In addition, there seem to be a number of people in our political and journalistic world for whom a certain Cold War rhetoric has long been the staff of life, who have been alarmed by an apparent favorable trend in our relationship to Russia that has threatened to undermine the basis for this rhetoric, and who now welcome the chance to attack that trend. The result has been the emergence of a school of thought which appears to believe that something useful could now be achieved in our relations with Russia by a policy of strident hostility on our part, by reversion to the Cold War slogans of the fifties, by calling names and making faces, by piling up still greater quantities of superfluous armaments, and by putting public pressure on Moscow to change its internal practices, and indeed the very nature of Soviet power.

George F. Kennan, *The Nuclear Delusion*, 1976.

This method, on the face of it, was breathtakingly simple: containment would be made to work better at less cost by reducing the number of threats to be contained....

Détente,...was hardly an abandonment of containment, as its critics have charged. It was, rather, an imaginative effort to accommodate that strategy to existing realities, to maintain that calculated relationship of ends and means that any strategy must have in order to succeed. "We did not consider a relaxation of tensions a concession to the Soviets," Kissinger has recalled. "We had our own reasons for it. We were not abandoning the ideological struggle, but simply trying—tall order as it was—to discipline it by precepts of the national interest." And, again: "Détente defined not friendship but a strategy for a relationship among adversaries."...

In some respects, this strategy of seeking containment by way of détente succeeded remarkably well. The SALT I agreements did limit significant aspects of the strategic arms race. Chronic issues perpetuating cold war tensions in Europe, notably Berlin, were now defused. Détente reversed, with deceptive ease, long-standing patterns of hostility by building a cooperative relationship with the Chinese at the expense of the Russians. Soviet power in the Middle East declined dramatically at a time when the dependence of Western economies on that part of the world was growing. Détente brought the Russians themselves into a position of economic dependence on the West that had not been present before. And, above all, détente ended Washington's myopic fixation with what Kissinger called "a small peninsula on a major continent"— Vietnam—and focused its attention back on more important global concerns. It is no small tribute to the architects of détente—though one should not deny credit as well to the clumsiness of the Russians—that by any index of power other than military, the influence and prestige of the United States compared to that of the Soviet Union was significantly greater at the beginning of the 1980s than it had been a decade earlier.

A Misunderstanding of Détente

Despite these achievements, though, détente by 1980 was almost universally regarded as having failed. The Russians had surged ahead of the United States in both strategic and conventional military power, it was argued. They had tightened rather than loosened controls on their own people. They had continued efforts to destabilize Third World areas; they had violated solemn agreements and, of course, most conspicuously, in 1979, they had brutally invaded Afghanistan. If this was containment, critics asked, could appeasement be far behind?

To some extent, these charges reflect a misunderstanding of what détente was all about in the first place. As we have seen, it was never intended entirely to end the arms race, or to eliminate competitions for influence in the Third World, or to serve as an instrument of reform within the Soviet Union, although official hyperbole at times gave that impression in the early 1970s. Rather, it sought to provide mechanisms for managing conflicts among adversaries, thereby lowering the dangers of escalation and overcommitment without at the same time compromising vital interests....

100

Containment will no doubt remain the central focus of our strategy in world affairs for some years to come. The Soviet Union shows no signs of contenting itself with the existing distribution of power in the world; experience certainly should have taught us by now that our capacity to moderate Moscow's ambitions by any means other than some fairly crude combination of sticks and carrots is severely limited. Still, there are a few things we might learn from our experience with containment to this point; things any future administration might do well to keep in mind as it seeks to devise strategies for dealing with the Russians.

The president and his men discuss the failures of peacekeeping.

Mike Lane for the *Evening Sun*. Reprinted with permission.

One is precisely how little we have learned from the past....Has the time not come to attempt to build into our policy-formulation process some sense of what has gone before, and at least of what elementary conclusions might be derived from it? There are various ways in which this might be accomplished: one might establish a permanent nonpartisan staff for the National Security Council, the only key policymaking body in this field that does not now have one; one might draw in a more formal and systematic capacity than is now done upon the expertise of retired presidents, national security advisors, secretaries of state and other experienced "elder" statesmen; one might even take the drastic step of encouraging high officials actually to read history themselves from time to time. The point would be to get away from our amnesiac habit of periodically re-inventing the wheel; after all, the general shape of that device is reasonably well understood and may not need to be re-thought with each revolution....

We could also learn to be more precise about just what it is we are out to contain. Is the adversary the Soviet Union? Is it the world communist movement? It is the great variety of non-communist Marxist movements that exist throughout the world? Surely in an era in which we rely upon the world's most populous communist state to help contain the world's most powerful communist state, in an era when some of our best friends are socialists, there can be little doubt about the answer to this question. And yet, as our current policy in Central America and the Caribbean shows, we persist in lumping together the Soviet Union, international communism, and non-communist Marxism in the most careless and imprecise manner—to what end? It is a fundamental principle of strategy that one should never take on any more enemies than necessary at any given point. But we seem to do it all the time.

Using Nationalism

It follows from this that we could also make greater use than we do of our friends. Most other nations heartily endorse our goal of a world safe for diversity; few, given the choice, would align themselves with the quite different goals of the Russians. Nationalism, in short, works for us rather than against us. And yet, we seem to go out of our way, at times, to alienate those who would cooperate in the task of containment. The blank check we have extended to the Israelis over the years—however useful in producing occasional grudging concessions on their part—has nonetheless impaired our ability to make common cause with the other nations of the Middle East whose interests we largely share: that the Russians have been able to take so little advantage of this situation is more a testimony to their ineptitude than to our wisdom. Our support for Taiwan for years prevented any exploitation of the Sino-Soviet split, and to this day retains the potential for weakening our very important relationship with mainland China. Our attitude toward white minority regimes in southern Africa has not always been best calculated to win us influence in the rest of that continent, most of whose leaders emphatically share our desire to keep the Russians out....Containment would function more efficiently if others shared some of the burden of containing. And yet, we sometimes seem to make that difficult.

Another trick that would make containment work better would be to take advantage, to a greater extent than we have, of the Russians' chronic tendency to generate resistance to themselves. This is one reason why Moscow has not been able to exploit the opportunities we have handed them in the Middle East and Africa; it is why they have such difficulty consolidating opportunities they have taken advantage of themselves, as in Afghanistan. It is a cliché, by now, to describe the Soviet Union as the last great imperial power; what is not a cliché, but rather one of the more reliable "lessons" to be drawn from the admittedly imprecise discipline of history, is that imperial powers ultimately wind up containing themselves through the resistance they themselves provoke. Nothing could be clearer than that this is happening to the Russians today, and yet we seem not to take it much into account in framing our policies. We should.

Cooling the Rhetoric

It would also help if we would cool the rhetoric. The [Reagan] Administration is hardly the first to engage in verbal overkill, but the frequency and vividness of its excesses in this regard surely set some kind of record. The President has informed us that Jesus—not Kennan—was the original architect of containment. The Vice President has...criticized not only Soviet but Tsarist Russia for arrested cultural development, pointing out (with some historic license) that that country took no part in the Renaissance, the Reformation or the Enlightenment; this would appear to be the diplomatic equivalent of saying: "Yeah, and so's your old man!" These are childish, but not innocent, pleasures. They demean those who engage in them, and therefore dignify the intended target. They obscure the message: how many people will recall Ambassador Charles Lichenstein's eloquent and amply deserved condemnation of the Korean airliner atrocity once he had coupled it with his offer to stand on the docks, waving goodbye to the United Nations? That the Russians themselves have long been masters of the art of invective is no reason to try to emulate them; this is one competition in which we can safely allow their preeminence.

Finally, and in this connection, we should keep in mind the ultimate objectives of containment. That strategy was and still should be the means to a larger end, not an end in itself. It should lead to something; otherwise, like any strategy formulated without reference to policy, it is meaningless. There is a tendency in this country to let means become ends, to become so preoccupied with processes that one loses sight of the goal those processes were supposed to produce. We have been guilty of that to some extent with containment; we have missed in the past and are probably today still missing opportunities to manage, control, and possibly resolve many of our disagreements with the Russians, apparently out of fear that such contacts might weaken the public's resolve to support containment. But that is getting things backward. The original idea of containment was ultimately to facilitate, not impede, the attainment of a less dangerous international order. It would not be a bad idea—from the point of view of everybody's interests—to get back to that concept....

Given all the impediments that exist in our society to the rational formulation of strategy, what is remarkable is not that we have done less well than we might have these past three and a half decades, but that we have done it at all. Containment has, on the whole, been a successful strategy, despite all its imprecisions, inefficiencies, and inconsistencies. One reason for this is that we have been fortunate in our antagonists—the Russians have been even more inept than we in seeking to promote their interests in the world.

"There is not an instant when [communism] does not think of the non-Communist world as an enemy to be destroyed, while the democracies imagine they can buy peace by conceding communism a share of the globe."

Peaceful Coexistence Is Impossible

Jean-Francois Revel

Democratic capitalist society and Soviet communism cannot co-exist, according to the author of the following viewpoint, Jean-Francois Revel, a well-known French philosopher and journalist. Communism is a failure as an economic system, Mr. Revel argues, and the Soviets must continually expand since they cannot solve the internal problems they have created. The Soviets remember the West's inconsistent policies of trying to contain communism and then making concessions. Mr. Revel concludes that they use such lessons to expand even farther, at democracy's expense.

As you read, consider the following questions:

1. How does Mr. Revel counter the argument that the internal problems Soviet communism has created will lead to its downfall?
2. In Mr. Revel's opinion, how have the Soviets used Western capitalists to help their ailing economy?
3. What reasons does Mr. Revel give for the Soviets' skill at foreign policy and the West's ineptitude?

Democratic civilization is the first in history to blame itself because another power is working to destroy it. The distinguishing mark of our century is not so much communism's determination to erase democracy from our planet, or its frequent success in pursuing that end, as it is the humility with which democracy is not only consenting to its own obliteration but is contriving to legitimize its deadiest enemy's victory.

It is natural for communism to try with all its might to eliminate democracy, since the two systems are incompatible and communism's survival depends on its rival's annihilation. That the Communist offensive is more successful, more skillful than democracy's resistance will be seen by history as just another example of one power outmaneuvering another. But it is less natural and more novel that the stricken civilization should not only be deeply convinced of the rightness of its own defeat, but that it should regale its friends and foes with reasons why defending itself would be immoral and, in any event, superfluous, useless, even dangerous.

Extravagant Criticism

Civilizations losing confidence in themselves: an old story in history. They stop believing they can survive, because of an internal crisis that is both insoluble and intolerable or under threat from an external enemy so strong that the civilization must choose between servitude and suicide. I do not believe democracy is in either predicament, but it acts as if it were in both. What distinguishes it is its eagerness to believe in its own guilt and its inevitable result. Democracy's predecessors hid such beliefs as shameful even when they thought, or knew, they were doomed. But democracy is zealous in devising arguments to prove the justice of its adversary's case and to lengthen the already overwhelming list of its own inadequacies....

Exaggerated self-criticism would be a harmless luxury of civilization if there were no enemy at the gate condemning democracy's very existence. But it becomes dangerous when it portrays its mortal enemy as always being in the right. Extravagant criticism is a good propaganda device in internal politics. But if it is repeated often enough, it is finally believed. And where will the citizens of democratic societies find reasons to resist the enemy outside if they are persuaded from childhood that their civilization is merely an accumulation of failures and a monstrous imposture? At both ends of the democratic world's political spectrum there is agreement with the Soviet Union's rationale for its plan to destroy the liberal societies—from radical critics out of conviction, from conservatives out of resignation.

While the principle of political democracy may no longer be contested from within, it is under worldwide attack as it has never before been in its brief history. And that attack, which is being waged with unexampled vigor, scope and intelligence, is catching the democracies in a state of intellectual impotence and political indolence that disposes them to defeat and makes a Communist victory probable, if not inevitable.

It is also possible that democratic civilization will not die forever, that it is merely at the close of a cycle, the end of a first period of individual freedoms as modern democracy understands them....

Soviet Internal Problems

There is a widespread belief that a society's survival depends on its ability to satisfy its members' needs. Relying on this notion, many Western leaders and commentators point to the chronic anemia of the Soviet economy, which seems not only to be irremediable but to be growing steadily worse, and see in it the imminent collapse of the Soviet empire, or at least a forced slowdown of its expansionary momentum.

Others, however, find cause for alarm for the democracies in communism's extraordinary incompetence: unrelieved internal failure, they fear, drives the empire's masters to seek external success. I hasten to add that whichever of the two theories is favored, Western governments' conclusion is that the Soviet Union must be appeased. If it is true that the Soviet imperialist drive is slowing down for lack of fuel, why whip it up with tough diplomacy? And if its temper is being darkened by internal bankruptcy, wouldn't Western inflexibility provoke a disproportionately violent Soviet reaction? Do we want them to blow up the planet?...

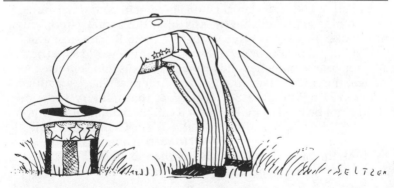

Isadore Seltzer for *The Nation*. Reprinted with permission.

The idea that an authoritarian political system must collapse because it cannot provide a decent life for its citizenry can only occur to a democrat. When we reason this way about the Soviet empire, we are simply ascribing democracy's operational rules and attitudes to a totalitarian regime. But these rules and attitudes are signally abnormal and, as I said earlier, very recent and probably transitory. The notion that whoever holds power must clear out because his subjects are discontented or dying of hunger or distress is a bit of whimsy that history has tolerated wondrously few times in real life....How could totalitarian rulers break a social contract they've never signed?

As things stand, relatively minor causes of discontent corrode, disturb, unsettle, paralyze the democracies faster and more deeply than horrendous famine and constant poverty do the Communist regimes, whose subject peoples have no real rights or means of redressing their wrongs. Societies of which permanent criticism is an integral feature are the only livable ones, but they are also the most fragile. They will continue to be the most fragile as long as theirs is not the only system in the world and must compete with systems that do not burden themselves with the same obligations. We must not ascribe this kind of fragility to totalitarianism; it is exclusive to democracy, along with another kind that needs identifying....

Soviet expansion took its two longest forward leaps since the war at two moments when the West's guard was down or when the democracies were paralyzed. In 1945-50, taking advantage of the vacuum left by the rapid and thoroughly irresponsible departure of American forces from Europe, the Soviet Union imposed communism on all of Eastern and Central Europe except Austria. In 1975, the Vietnam debacle and the removal from office of President Richard M. Nixon left the United States cataleptic. Western Europe, sprawled on the sofa of détente, ecstatic over America's humiliation and over the Helsinki agreement, was determined to see nothing reprehensible in anything the Soviet Union might undertake. In less than five years, the U.S.S.R., the strongest but one of the Asiatic European powers, became a world superpower, spreading stout branches and promising shoots into Southeast Asia, Africa, the Middle East and Central America. These gigantic advances exemplified the Soviet precept that military superiority should not be used to make war if it can be avoided but to impose the U.S.S.R.'s will without a fight. It's a Communist rule the Western Europeans would do well to keep in mind. They are wrong to think the only alternative facing them is invasion by the Red Army or total freedom. Conditional liberty is also a possibility....

Observing Precedents

The conduct of any policy, domestic or international, cannot and should not be wholly a prisoner of precedent. Divorcing oneself from the past can be the best or the worst of things—the best when it eliminates analysis of obsolete elements so as to center action on current ones, but worst when it amounts to a complacent forgetfulness of the lessons of history that can lead to the repetition of old mistakes. Failing to realize that he is facing a new situation is a serious error for a diplomat. But not recognizing an old situation in which he'd been bested before is still more unpardonable.

This is a mistake the Soviets rarely commit. They remember all the West's reactions and lack of reactions—let's say the adversary's, rather, for they never stop regarding us as the adversary, even in periods of so-called peaceful coexistence. Moscow knows the ruts the democracies invariably fall into when faced with a challenge. Their reaction is more often disarray and renunciation than counterthrust and injunction. Moscow knows this; it registered the fact in connection with the oil crisis that began in 1973, with Soviet-Cuban expansion in Africa, after its sabotage of the Helsinki agree-

---

Red Terror

Lenin issued the following directive...to his secret police: "We are not waging war against separate individuals; we are exterminating the bourgeoisie as a class....Do not ask for incriminating evidence to prove that the prisoner opposed the Soviet government either by arms or word. Your first duty is to ask him what class he belongs to, what were his origin, education, and occupation. These questions should decide the fate of the prisoner. This is the meaning and essence of Red Terror."

Which is something for those who think the Communists will leave them alone, if only they do nothing to oppose Communism, to keep in mind.

Robert W. Lee, *American Opinion*, November 1983.

---

ment, after the Iranian revolution, with the civil wars in Central America, and in the disputes that followed the repression in Poland. They also know that since 1921 the Soviet economy has periodically been rescued by Western aid; these are concrete actions that far outweigh all the anti-Communist rhetoric the Kremlin hears. They know their deceits and aggressions have never met with lasting reprisals from the West, not even with cancellation of its financial and technological assistance. They know these things and, what's more, they know the West does not know them, that Western public opinion and even the West's governors have forgotten them and will continue to forget them. This allows the Soviets to count on the West's trust, indefinitely forthcoming, renewed and renewable whenever Moscow chooses to repeat its old tricks.

Hoodwinked Capitalists

The main lines of the Soviet diplomatic offensives were fixed in the early years of the Communist regime. The intellectual framework of proposals the West sees as new every time it reappears was assembled long ago by the Soviets, along with the techniques by which they milk all their agreements with the West for unilateral advantages. To us, there was the eternal freshness of novelty in our disputes beginning in 1970 about whether to seek economic détente and, in the 1980s, about whether to go on seeking it. But seen from the Soviet side, economic cooperation was simply an example of a proven old formula: "We greatly need technical assistance from the United States and Canada....If the Americans keep their promises, the benefit for us will be enormous....Agreement with and concessions to the Americans are exceptionally important to us....I consider it enormously important to attract American capital to build...the pipeline in Georgia. Hammer's son (and partner) is in Russia. He has been in the Urals and has decided to restore industry there....Shouldn't Hammer also be interested in the electrification plan so that he may supply not only our bread, but electrical equipment as well (on credit, of course)?...With the Germans, the tightening of trade relations is going well. With Italy, it is beginning; she has offered us a loan...."

These lines date from 1921! They were taken from notes Lenin sent to members of the Politburo and to Molotov and Mikhailov, the two secretaries of the Central Committee. They show that, very early on, Soviet leaders were extremely clear on their goals, namely, to get the capitalist countries to come to the aid of the Soviet economy whenever it is ailing, if possible at their own expense, and in any case on credit terms so favorable as to border on subsidy. In exchange, the capitalist countries were to be satisfied either with their own naive faith in the miraculous democratization of communism through the gentle virtues of trade or with promises of restraint in foreign policy that the U.S.S.R. has never kept or intended to keep, as it has almost always admitted, with admirable cynicism, in the most thinly veiled terms. Doesn't it know in advance that the Western countries would forget their previous mortifications, that they would jubilantly rush to resume their old roles as hoodwinked benefactors if only Moscow took the trouble to spruce up a few of its old promises?

Reasons for Soviet Success

This is what happened in 1921, in 1928, in 1947, and especially beginning in 1970. Its record of past experience and its perspicacious vision of the future, based of course on the West's combined amnesia and myopia, enabled Moscow to nip in the bud any Western attempt at linkage, that is, subordination of economic aid to Soviet foreign-policy restraint, stabilization of the Soviet empire, and an end to destabilization in other countries....

If Soviet diplomacy is successful, it is not because the men in the Kremlin are endowed with any particular genius. It is because they stick to a method that includes the principles of long-term continuity of action, constant review of the reasons for that action, and acceptance of the fact that solid, irreversible results can be slow in coming. On the other hand, Western diplomacy, however intelligent its practitioners (intelligence that, more often than not, shines outside of politics), is discontinuous. Leadership changes frequently, and the new teams tend to forget or mistrust the reasoning behind their predecessor's decisions. And the democracies' diplomacy is guided by a need to feed public opinion with quick, spectacular results. The upshot of all this is that Western diplomacy is more easily led by the nose than Soviet diplomacy is. Moscow wins the advantage over the long haul, a fact Westerners refuse to believe; to them, the idea that everything the Soviets do is the fruit of long-term calculations is a sign of paranoia....

Communist Hostility

The main goal of Communism is an irrational and fanatical urge to swallow the maximum amount of external territory and population, with the ideal limit being the entire planet. Under Communism a country is never prepared for a long and healthy economic existence. But it is always ready to strike, to seize, and to expand militarily—that is an indispensable mode of Communist existence....Marxism is hostile to the physical existence and the spiritual essence of every nation. It is futile to hope that a compromise with Communism will be found, or that relations will be inproved by concessions and trade....

To improve or to correct Communism is not feasible. Communism can only be done away with—by the joint efforts of the many peoples oppressed by it.

Aleksandr Solzhenitsyn, *National Review*, January 21, 1983.

There is nothing original about exploiting an adversary's weaknesses and seeking out his vulnerable spots. Communism scores its points because it thinks of nothing else, whereas the democracies' concentration is negligent, intermittent, changeable. Communism also advances because there is not an instant when it does not think of the non-Communist world as an enemy to be destroyed, while the democracies imagine they can buy peace by conceding communism a share of the globe. They forget that communism cannot allow itself to stop. It expands or it dies, since it cannot solve any of the internal problems of the societies it creates....

Long-Range Vision

For the past forty years, the democracies, seeking what they thought should be a durable global balance, have always been ready to make concessions to the Soviet Union to prove their goodwill and oblige it to show its own. The trouble is that all these treaties, which the West sees as domes of stability, are viewed by the Communists as springboards for destabilization. Communism is not at all interested in replacing the race toward domination with a race toward civilization that it knows it would be doomed to lose. It is greedy for treaties too, but only to receive guarantees, not to give them. A pact is hardly signed before the Communists' active vigilance sends them back on the attack, exploiting the clauses favorable to them and crossing out the others. Everyone is aware of their violations of the Helsinki agreement. But we tend to forget that after World War II Stalin lost no time at all before violating the treaties designed to ''rebuild'' the postwar world, the agreements signed in Teheran (December 1943), Yalta (February 1945), and Potsdam (August 1945). All the armistice conventions, the interallied agreements, the peace treaties with Germany, Poland, Hungary, Bulgaria, Romania, Korea were broken by the Soviets. Only Austria escaped, a miraculous survivor of the great Soviet sweep, and so did Finland, a semisatellite with a special status. In the same way, the 1973 cease-fire in Indochina was immediately violated by the Communists; North Vietnam's armored divisions completed the conquest of South Vietnam in 1975.

Long-Range Visions

We are dealing here with two kinds of long-range vision. The democracies' is based in law and relies chiefly for respect of that law on the parties' sincerity and pragmatic restraint. The Communists consider nothing but the balance of power and see treaties merely as one of the many ways to lull their adversaries' already somnolent vigilance for a while. When the Soviet Union and the Communist International are in a superior position, they hasten to press their advantage, ignoring treaties; if they are in an inferior position, they fall back temporarily before attacking again as soon as they can. What is more, each phase of a Communist operation is held in reserve, no matter how long the forced interruption, until it can again be connected to the one that follows. Eventually, the past is welded into the general framework of a program that, unlike the democracies', is never left uncompleted.

112

3 VIEWPOINT

"The Soviet Union has continued to carry on the fight for complete and universal disarmament, for the banning of nuclear weapons forever, and for every partial step in this direction."

The Soviet Union Promotes Peace

Jessica Smith

Jessica Smith was formerly editor of the *New World Review*. In the following viewpoint taken from an editorial by Ms. Smith, she outlines what she considers to be some of the major peace efforts undertaken by the Soviet Union in this century. Communist Russia, she concludes, should be saluted by a war-weary world for standing "in the vanguard of the fight for peace."

As you read, consider the following questions:

1. According to the author, what are some of the positive peace achievements for which the Soviet Union has been responsible since World War II?
2. What was Lenin's "Decree of Peace"?

Jessica Smith, "The USSR and the Socialist World in the Struggle for Peace," *New World Review*, April 1974. Reprinted with permission.

The very first foreign policy act of the young Soviet Government, on November 8, 1917, was Lenin's Decree of Peace, along with decrees ending exploitation of man by man and people by people within its own country and of exploitation of nation by nation in its relations with other countries. The Decree of Peace was firmly grounded in the establishment of the new society in which no group, no monopolies existed to profit from the means of war, and which needed peace above all for the building of socialism. Lenin's Decree of Peace demonstrated that a main aim of socialism is to eliminate war from the life of mankind....

While the Soviet Union was initiating disarmament and other proposals to maintain peace among the nations on a world scale it was likewise busily pursuing peaceful bilateral diplomatic relations which had been achieved with most of the nations of the world. In this the US lagged behind the other big powers, ceaselessly carrying on anti-Soviet actions and propaganda for 16 years, with the hope of somehow erasing the first socialist society from the earth by refusing to recognize its existence. With the accession of Franklin D. Roosevelt to the Presidency diplomatic relations were finally established, in November, 1933.

As the fascist danger in Europe rose menacingly, with Nazi Germany rearming and uniting with Mussolini in its agressive plans, and with Japan resorting to war on China and preparing for war on the Soviet Union, the USSR continued to reaffirm its peace and disarmament policy at the Geneva Disarmament Conference. It proposed that the Disarmament Conference be transformed into a permanent peace conference joined by all nations, for the prevention of war....

The Postwar Period

Throughout the postwar period the Soviet Union has continued to carry on the fight for complete and universal disarmament, for the banning of nuclear weapons forever, and for every partial step in this direction. Its peace efforts, through the UN and every other medium, are at their very height today.

The UN Charter which was signed in San Francisco June 26, 1945, and came into force the following October 24, sought to set up a realistic structure and machinery "to maintain international peace and security, to take collective measures for prevention and removal of threats to peace," and in general, under Article I, "To be a center for the harmonizing of the actions of nations for these common ends." The Soviet Union played an important role in working out these aims and in carrying them out ever since.

The cold war, soon started against the Soviet Union and the new socialist countries that came into being in the postwar period, hampered the operations of the world body for many years. In recent years we have seen the tide turning as the UN achieves greater universality, with the influence of the Soviet Union and the socialist states in world affairs growing ever stronger and the important new addition of most of the former colonial nations, whose independence was owed in great part to the example and aid of the Soviet Union and the socialist sector of the world. Desperate efforts were made to fasten the blame for the cold war on the Soviet Union....

Soviet Deliverance

The foreign policy of the Soviet Union, together with that of other socialist countries, is aimed at securing favorable international condition....upholding consistently the principle of the peaceful coexistence of states with different social systems, firmly repelling the aggressive forces of imperialism and delivering mankind from the threat of a new world war.

William J. Pomeroy, *New World Review*, December, 1975.

Fortunately a whole series of "revisionist" historians have been setting the record straight, beginning with D. F. Fleming's authoritative and well-documented *The Cold War and Its Origins.* This and numerous other books have made clear that there has never been any threat of aggression from the Soviet Union, and that the real criminals were the "Western Democracies" themselves....

Soviet Peace Proposals

In 1959 the Soviet Union made the first postwar proposal for general and complete disarmament when Premier Khrushchev presented a detailed declaration for consideration by the UN Assembly. The Soviet proposals were warmly welcomed by many UN members and remained on the agenda. As a result of the Soviet proposals, the 18-nation UN Disarmament Commmittee (later enlarged) was set up at Geneva; this committee has since been working on partial disarmament steps and has achieved a series of important results, all based mainly on Soviet initiative and supported by the socialist community of nations, as follows:

• A treaty barring armaments and nuclear tests in the Antarctic (1959)

• A treaty prohibiting military activities in outer space (1967).

• A treaty making Latin America an atom-free zone (1967).

• A treaty prohibiting proliferation of nuclear weapons to additional countries (1968).

• A treaty banning emplacement of weapons of mass destruction on the ocean floor (1971).

• A convention on prohibition of the development, production and stockpiling of bacteriological (biological) and toxic weapons and on their destruction (1972).

It should be noted that in all the above cases the Soviet Union has continued to work on further expanding the agreements and on their complete implementation. For example, it continues to seek agreement on cessation of *all* nuclear weapons tests, including underground. Unable to reach agreement on banning of chemical weapons because of US opposition, the USSR finally agreed to the ban on bacteriological weapons with the provision that the negotiations on banning chemical weapons as well be continued....

Recent Peace Efforts

Recent years have seen an acceleration and intensification of Soviet initiatives in every area bearing on curbing the arms race and easing tensions between nations. Each fall, when Soviet Foreign Minister Andre Gromyko has attended the opening UN General Assembly sessions, he has had a new special proposal for the agenda. The struggle is carried on throughout the session by Ambassador Malik, permanent representative, with the support of other socialist member nations, among which only Albania, and China since its admission in 1971, have been opposed....

Much has been accomplished in the general easing of world tensions by the personal visits of General Secretary Brezhnev to many countries, and especially the historic US-USSR Summit meetings in 1973 and 1974. We cannot overestimate the significance of the joint statement of basic principles made in Moscow when the new world situation and the low estate reached by our own country forced President Nixon into the recognition that for the US and the USSR, "in the nuclear age there is no alternative to conducting their mutual relations on the basis of peaceful co-existence." Of equally vital importance was the landmark agreement in Washington on the prevention of nuclear war, and the whole complex of cooperative agreements between our countries....

We know our readers will wish to join us...in saluting the great nation that is in the vanguard of the fight for peace, the members of the socialist community of nations who march beside it, and the many peoples of the world who are swelling the ranks of the partisans of peace.

4

"The Communist ideology is to destroy your society. This has been their aim for 125 years and has never changed."

The Soviet Union Promotes Conflict

Aleksandr Solzhenitsyn

Aleksandr Solzhenitsyn is perhaps the most famous and controversial Soviet expatriate in the world today. Expelled from the Soviet Union in 1974, Mr. Solzhenitsyn's life as a Soviet citizen was marked by trial and misfortune. He served as commander of a Russian artillery battery during WW II and was twice decorated for bravery. Immediately after the war, however, Mr. Solzhenitsyn was imprisoned from 1945 to 1953 for writing a letter critical of Soviet dictator Joseph Stalin and then was exiled to Siberia from 1953 to 1956. Officially "rehabilitated" in 1957, he taught mathe-

Excerpted from Aleksandr Solzhenitsyn, "Detente and Democracy," *Society*, November-December, 1975. Published by permission of Transaction, Inc. from *Society*, Vol. 13 #1. Copyright © 1975 by Transaction, Inc.

matics at a secondary school in Ryaza, Russia, during which time he was admitted to the Union of Soviet Writers. Mr. Solzhenitsyn was expelled from the writers' union in 1969 when his unrelenting attacks upon the Soviet government, its policies, and leadership began to prove dangerous and embarrassing. Winner of the Nobel Prize for Literature in 1970, his criticism of the Soviet Union has intensified since his exile. In the following viewpoint, Mr. Solzhenitsyn expresses doubt that peaceful coexistence with Communist Russia is possible at this time. He warns that communism has advocated the destruction of Western society for the past 125 years and that that policy remains unchanged.

Four years after being refused permission to leave Russia, Solzhenitsn receives his Nobel Prize for literature.

United Press International, Inc.

As you read, consider the following questions:

1. According to the author, why did the Communists reverse their position on peaceful coexistence?
2. Why does the author believe that "there will not be any nuclear war"?
3. What does the author mean by the following: "Communism ...rejects all absolute concepts of morality"?

Communism is as crude an attempt to explain society and the individual as if a surgeon were to perform his delicate operations with a meat-ax. All that is subtle in human psychology and in the structure of society (which is even more delicate); all of this is reduced to crude economic processes. This whole created being—man—is reduced to matter. It's characteristic that communism is so devoid of arguments that it has none to advance against its opponents in our Communist countries. It lacks arguments and hence there is the club, the prison, the concentration camp, and insane asylums with forced confinement....

Communist Morality

Communism has never concealed the fact that it rejects all absolute concepts of morality. It scoffs at any consideration of "good" and "evil" as indisputable categories. Communism considers morality to be too relative to be a class matter. Depending upon circumstances and the political situation, any act, including murder, even the killing of thousands, could be good or could be bad. It all depends upon class ideology. And who defines class ideology? The whole class cannot get together to pass judgment. A handful of people determine what is good and what is bad....Communism has managed to instill in all of us that these concepts are old-fashioned concepts and laughable. But if we are to be deprived of the concepts of good and evil, what will be left? Nothing but the manipulation of one another. We will decline to the status of animals.

Both the theory and practice of communism are completely inhuman for that reason....

But what is amazing is that apart from all their books, communism has offered a multitude of examples for modern man to see. The tanks have rumbled through Budapest. It is nothing. The tanks roar into Czechoslovakia. It is nothing. No one else would have been forgiven, but communism can be excused. With some kind of strange deliberation, as though God wanted to punish them by taking away their reason, the Communists erected the Berlin wall. It is indeed a monstrous symbol that demonstrates the true meaning of communism. For 14 years people have been machine gunned there....

The Question of War

The question of war is also well elucidated in Communist and Marxist literature. Let me show you how communism regards the question of war. I quote Lenin: "We cannot support the slogan 'Peace' since we regard it as a totally muddled one and a hindrance to the revolutionary struggle." (Letter to Alexandra Kollontai, July 1915.) "To reject war in principle is un-Marxist. Who objectively stands to gain from the slogan 'Peace'? In any case not the revolutionary proletariat." (Letter to Alexander G. Shliapnikov, November 1914.) "There's no point in proposing a benign program of pious wishes for peace without at the same time placing at the forefront the call for illegal organization and the summons to Civil War." This is communism's view of war. War is necessary. War is an instrument for achieving a goal.

But unfortunately for communism, this policy ran up against your atomic bomb in 1945. The American atomic bomb. Then the Communists changed their tactics. Then they suddenly became advocates of peace at any cost. They started to convoke peace congresses, to circulate petitions for peace, and the western world fell for this deceit. But the goal, the ideology, remained the same. To destroy your society. To destroy the way of life known in the West.

But with your nuclear superiority, it wasn't possible to do this then. Hence they replaced one concept with another. They said: what is not war is peace. That is to say, they opposed war to peace. But this was a mistake. Only a part of the antithesis opposed to the thesis. Although an open war could not be conducted, they could still carry out their oppressions behind the scene—terrorism. Partisan war, violence, prisons, concentration camps. I ask you: is this peace?

The Cult of Violence

In Communist revolutions, force and violence are a condition for further development and even progress. In the words of earlier revolutionaries, force and violence were only a necessary evil and a means to an end. In the words of Communists, force and violence are elevated to the lofty position of a cult and an ultimate end.

Milovan Djilas, *The New Class.*

The diametric opposite of peace is violence. And those who want peace in the world should remove not only war from the world, but also violence. If there is no open war, but there is still violence, that is not peace.

As long as in the Soviet Union, in China, and in other Communist countries there's no limit to the use of violence...as long as nothing restrains the use of violence over this tremendous land mass (more than half of humanity), how can you consider yourselves secure...?

The Communist ideology is to destroy your society. This has been their aim for 125 years and has never changed; only the methods have changed a little. When there is détente, peaceful co-existence, and trade, they will still insist: the ideological war must continue! And what is ideological war? It is a focus of hatred, this is continued repetition of the oath to destroy the western world....

The principal argument of the advocates of détente is...to avoid a nuclear war. But after all that has happened in recent years, I think I can set their minds at ease...there will not be any nuclear war. What for? Why should there be a nuclear war if for the last 30 years they have been breaking off as much of the West as they wanted—piece after piece, country after country and the process keeps going on. In 1975 alone four countries were broken off. Four—three in Indochina plus India, the process keeps going on, and very rapidly, too....

'I DON'T HEAR ANY SCREECHING BRAKES'

Don Hesse ©1977 *St. Louis Globe Democrat.* Reprinted with permission from the L.A. Times Syndicate.

At one time there was no comparison between the strength of the USSR and yours. Then it became equal to yours. Now, as all recognize, it is becoming superior to yours. Perhaps today the ratio is just greater than equal, but soon it will be 2 to 1. Then 3 to 1. Finally it will be 5 to 1....With such a nuclear superiority it will be possible to block the use of your weapons, and on some unlucky morning they will declare: "Attention. We're marching our troops to Europe, and if you make a move, we will annihilate you." And this ratio of 3 to 1, or 5 to 1 will have its effect: you will not make a move....

The Cold War—the war of hatred—is still going on, but only on the Communist side. What is the Cold War? It's a war of abuse and they still abuse you. They trade with you, they sign agreements and treaties, but they still abuse you, they still curse you. In sources which you can read, and even more in those which are unavailable to you, and which you don't hear of, in the depths of the Soviet Union, the Cold War has never stopped. It hasn't stopped for one second. They never call you anything but "American imperialists...."

A Friendly Handshake

In ancient times trade would begin with the meeting of two persons who had come out of a forest or had arrived by sea. They would show one another that they didn't have a stone or club in their hand, that they were unarmed. And as a sign of this each extended an open hand. This was the beginning of the hand clasp. Today's word "détente" literally means a reduction in the tension of a taut rope. (What an ominous coincidence: A rope again!)

So "détente means a relaxation of tension. But I would say that what we need is rather this image of the open hand. Relations between the Soviet Union and the United States of America should be such that there would be no deceit in the question of armaments, that there would be no concentration camps, no psychiatric wards for healthy people. Relations should be such that the throats of our women would no longer be constricted with tears, that there would be an end to the incessant ideological warfare waged against you....

This would be, I say, a period in which we would be able to present "open hands" to each other.

"Rather than seek to modify Soviet behavior, the West should assist those forces within the Communist bloc which are working for a change of the system."

US Policy Should Reform the Soviet System

Richard Pipes

Foreign policy analysts have long been faced with two choices for US policy toward the Soviets: either trying to change the Soviet system or trying to improve relations with the Soviets. Richard Pipes, the author of the following viewpoint, advocates the first strategy. Dr. Pipes is a historian at Harvard University and was director of the National Security Council in 1981-82. Soviet aggression is caused by the communist system itself, he argues, and Soviet behavior will not improve until the system is changed. By taking advantage of Soviet internal weaknesses, the West may be able to win the struggle with communism.

As you read, consider the following questions:

1. Why do the Soviets act aggressively, according to the author?
2. How, in the opinion of the author, have the Soviets taken advantage of domestic politics in the US to advance their global strategy?
3. How has the West helped the Soviet economic system become more efficient, according to Dr. Pipes?

Richard Pipes, "How to Cope with the Soviet Threat." Reprinted from *Commentary*, August 1984, by permission; all rights reserved.

U.S. global policy since World War II has tended to display an abstract and ideological quality: it has been less a defense of national interest than of a general international order. In dealing with the Soviet Union, U.S. policies strove above all to persuade it to join the international community by showing it that aggression did not pay, whereas restraint and cooperation did, inasmuch as the one brought rewards and the other punishments....

This kind of didactic diplomacy has been the basic premise of U.S. policy toward the USSR in times of the cold war as well as those of détente. Under this approach, the Soviet Union is treated rather as if it were a wayward child, which has to be taught proper manners by the application of pain and pleasure. Why the Soviet Union misbehaves—that is, acts aggressively—is a question which hardly anyone bothers to address, if one leaves aside the opinion of dilettante "experts" who believe that Russia has suffered an extraordinary number of foreign invasions and developed, as a consequence, a collective paranoia that expresses itself in aggression.

But this, surely, is the critical issue. Experience of the past sixty-seven years indicates that no attempt to influence Soviet behavior has succeeded: neither diplomatic ostracism, nor Yalta-like concessions, nor nuclear threats, nor economic bribery. This record of failure indicates that the cause of Soviet aggression lies deeper— that it is systemic. If this is the case, then it is vain to hope to modify Soviet behavior without modifications in the system which causes it.

The causes of Soviet aggressiveness are varied and many, some of them being rooted in Russian geography and history, others in Marxist-Leninist theory and practice. But perhaps the single most important of these causes resides in the fact that the Soviet Union and its dependencies are run by self-appointed and self-perpetuating elites whose extraordinary power, privileges, and wealth cannot be justified in any other way than by the alleged threat of "imperialist aggression" to the countries they rule. Their status is thus directly related to the level of international tension. They can best keep their restless subjects under control by demonstrating to them that Communist power is invincible, that it will eventually spread around the globe, and that, therefore, all resistance to it is futile. It is through aggression abroad that the Communist elite best safeguards its position at home....

International Relations Game

Rather than seek to modify Soviet *behavior*, the West should assist those forces within the Communist bloc which are working for a change of the *system*. This is best accomplished by refusing to play the game of international relations in the manner which Moscow prefers, and by denying it the opportunities to exploit military, political, and economic relations with the West to its own advantage. The West cannot destabilize the Soviet Union, but neither should it help the Soviet elite to stabilize a system which is increasingly strained by the incompatibility of the means at its disposal and the objectives which it pursues....

Soviet leaders...attach little importance to arms-control negotiations, except as they help to restrain *Western* advances in technology and to divide *Western* opinion. In internal Soviet literature on security issues, the subject is hardly ever mentioned. The USSR has not bothered even to establish a counterpart to the U.S. Arms Control and Disarmament Agency. Soviet personnel involved in these negotiations are dominated by the military, who, insofar as can be determined, are accountable to the General Staff, an institution not normally associated with disarmament. Evidence from SALT I, SALT II, and START negotiations suggests that the Soviet side first determines what weapons it requires to meet its strategic objectives and then concentrates on constraining, through negotiations, America's ability to respond. In the words of the French General Pierre Gallois, "[The Soviets] do what they want and negotiate about what you're going to do."

Marxist Militarism

Marxist regimes pursue military might....[as] an expression of their basic character, not [in] response to a particular foreign or domestic policy aim. One almost has to suppose that if a Marxist regime came to power on Mars, with nothing to conquer and nothing to defend against, it would still have an army twice as large as that of a comparable non-Marxist country here on Earth. The ruling parties in Marxist regimes reach for military power to validate their ideological view of a world locked in perpetual struggle. They have, as Henry Kissinger put it, "a vested interest in tension."

James L. Payne, *Wall Street Journal*, April 5, 1985.

The American experts who in 1972 concluded SALT I with the USSR did not believe in the military utility of nuclear weapons on either the strategic or the theater level. To them, an arms agreement was primarily a political device, the second pillar of détente (the other being credits and trade). As one European specialist put it at the time, "There's a lot of eyewash in these agreements, but their significance lies in the extent to which they reflect the mutual recognition of the need to cooperate in the nuclear-disarmament field." In other words, the terms did not matter as much as did the political atmospherics. From the beginning it was indeed the political process, cynically manipulated for its public-relations effect, rather than the deadly reality of the nuclear balance, that the U.S. and its allies regarded as the foremost priority. As a result of this attitude, the U.S. has allowed some very disadvantageous features to intrude into these accords, of which the public at large is quite ignorant.

The Soviet side has from the outset refused to furnish comprehensive data on its strategic systems—in itself a most extraordinary procedure. Since, however, negotiations on limiting numbers could not very well proceed without agreement on what these numbers were, Moscow has consented (without prejudice) to accept the data for its side furnished by the United States. The United States could account for only those Soviet systems of which it had solid evidence from its intelligence-gathering sources, not those that were beyond their scope. Although the Soviet Union subsequently agreed to furnish random data on its nuclear forces, the information at the disposal of the United States is certain to reflect only the minimum dimension of the Soviet nuclear arsenal; the precise dimensions of this arsenal were not and are not known. It would certainly be difficult to find a businessman prepared to enter into relations with a company that refused to provide him with complete information on its assets and debts; in the field of national security, unfortunately, different standards prevail....

Soviet Global Strategy

The chief instrument of Soviet global strategy is political attrition, which, in practice, means exploiting the open character of democratic societies for the purpose of inciting internal divisions among different social groups and between their citizens and their elected governments, as well as sowing discord among the allies. This strategy cannot be completely neutralized if only because democracies will not remain democracies once they disallow conflicts of interest and differences of opinion. But its pernicious effect can be significantly reduced when it is realized what it is and how it functions.

Ideally, political parties in democratic countries should seek to pursue a strictly bipartisan policy in regard to the Soviet Union. That such a policy is possible was demonstrated in the late 1940s and early 1950s in both the United States and West Germany. The breakdown of bipartisanship that has occurred subsequently as a result of the Soviet shift to "peaceful coexistence" provides Moscow with excellent opportunities to play on internal political rivalries in democratic countries by encouraging parties that are not in the least degree pro-Soviet or pro-Communist to assume, for narrow partisan interests, the positions it favors....

It is essential for the West not to allow Moscow to insinuate itself into its domestic politics and not to give it any opportunity for exploiting the "rifts" in the enemy camp which Lenin regarded as the prime objective of his political strategy. Not that there must be no disagreements in the Western camp, but rather that the West should instantly close ranks whenever the Soviet Union attempts to take part in them. Instead of giving Moscow such an opening, the West would do well to strike back and challenge the Soviet effort to seal off its domain from any outside interference. Through radio broadcasts (and, in the future, possibly television transmissions as well), through speeches of its statesmen, and through symbolic acts, it should be possible to raise in the minds of citizens of Communist countries doubts about the omnipotence of their regimes. To allow the Soviet Union to meddle in Western affairs but to desist from meddling in its affairs is to play into the hands of Soviet strategists.

The Soviet Union is even more successful in exploiting divisions in the Western alliance, whose cohesion, were it realizable, would constitute a most formidable obstacle to Soviet global ambitions....

The defensive ties binding the United States to Europe were, from the outset, territorially restricted to Europe, North America, and the Atlantic Ocean north of the Tropic of Cancer. This arrangement created serious problems because Soviet strategy is not regional but global in scope. The result was that all the areas outside the North Atlantic community came within the purview of other regional alliances tied to the United States but not to NATO: among them, the Baghdad Pact, SEATO, and the Rio Treaty. Inasmuch, however,

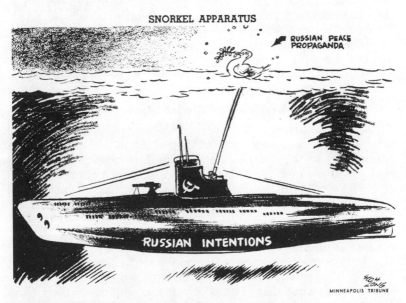

Reprinted with permission from the *Minneapolis Star and Tribune*.

as all regional defensive treaties except for NATO proved to be paper compacts, the United States has had to assume principal responsibility on its own behalf, as well as that of its European allies, for the security of the entire non-Western world outside the North Atlantic region.

Such an arrangement made sense in 1949, when NATO came into being, because at that time Europe was still incapable of insuring its own protection, let alone the defense of distant regions. Today it is difficult to justify either on grounds of equity or military expediency, for it imposes on the United States excessive burdens of protecting the approaches to Europe as well as coping with Soviet expansionism in the Third World. The defense of the Middle East, without whose oil Europe could hardly carry on, is entrusted to the United States, as is that of the mineral resources of Africa, not to speak of the strategic areas in East Asia and Central America. Whenever Communist forces commit acts of aggression in these outlying areas, Europe assumes the stance of a neutral observer. The detachment with which its leaders react to such events sometimes conveys the impression that they are not unhappy to have Russia dissipate its aggressive energies far away from the European continent. There seems little awareness in European thinking (a few honorable exceptions apart) that the Soviet Union pursues a global and not a continental strategy, that the invasion of Afghanistan has some bearing on the security of Europe's oil supplies, that a series of successful Communist revolutions in Central America may have the consequence of diverting American attention away from NATO. These matters, which do not happen to impinge on Europe's interests but affect its security in every other respect, are left to the care of the United States and such smaller non-European countries as Washington can persuade, bribe, or cajole into rendering it assistance.

The Heart of Soviet Strategy

An alliance, so inequitable in its principles and kept in place long after the circumstances that had shaped it have disappeared, is a monument to the short-sightedness of American diplomacy. It really is not so much an alliance as an insurance policy, extended by the United States to Western Europe at no expense to the insured but at an immense cost and risk to the insurer. As such, it offers Moscow superb opportunities for driving wedges between the U.S. and Western Europe. Moscow can, and does, deliberately exacerbate its differences with the United States, while offering "security" to Western Europe, so as to reduce artificially the East-West conflict to one that involves only the two "superpowers," which allegedly does not affect Europe's interests and from which it had best keep out. It heightens this effect by maintaining a stable East-West border in Europe and committing acts of aggression exclusively in regions outside the confines of NATO, where it runs into American but not European resistance. In this manner, Moscow succeeds in implementing the *divide et impera* principle which lies at the heart of its political strategy....

Bill Garner for the *Washington Times*. Reprinted with permission.

In the West it is widely believed that the Soviet economy is self-sufficient and that commercial relations with the West are an option that Moscow is at liberty to exercise or to reject. This assumption makes it possible to argue that there is no point in resorting to sanctions and embargoes to withhold equipment and technology from Communist states: the only effect such measures have is to push the Soviet Union toward autarky, to deprive Western firms of business, and to worsen the climate of international relations.

For all its popularity, this argument rests on a fallacious premise. Solid evidence that no one so far has been able to refute shows that the Soviet economy has never been self-sufficient and today is less so than ever. From 1921 on, almost without interruption, the USSR has been importing from the West significant quantities of materiel and know-how to modernize existing industries and to introduce new technology....

NATO long ago recognized the need to withhold from the USSR, and from countries likely to pass on to the USSR, equipment with obvious and direct military applications. In practice, enforcement of this principle has been hopelessly lax, especially since the inauguration of détente.

The agency charged with monitoring technology transfer to the

East is known by the acronym COCOM. Formed by NATO countries in 1949 with headquarters in Paris, and joined a few years later by Japan, COCOM maintains lists of embargoed technology, agreed upon by the allies. Alas, COCOM is virtually powerless to carry out its mandate. It is assigned an absurdly small budget (under $500,000 a year) with a correspondingly minuscule staff and can only recommend but not enforce its recommendations....

The sad reality is that while there are powerful vested interests lobbying for exports, no one has a vested interest in restricting the flow of technology to the potential enemy. Private enterprise does not seem especially concerned with who buys its product, as if oblivious of any connection between technology and military power; and governments lack the will to impose considerations higher than immediate profit on business. So it happens that while the West busily arms itself, it also helps arm its opponent....

Soviet Threat

The other objection to technology and equipment transfer has to do with its effect on the Stalinist system. Foreign technology and foreign credits help prop up an economic regime which shows every sign of having lost its vitality; they also enable Moscow to allocate its capital and resources in a manner that continues to favor the military sector. It is in the interest of the West that the USSR reform its labor policies, raising productivity by greater incentives and decentralized decision-making. This would represent a step toward weakening the economic and political power of the Soviet elite. To the extent that it helps to make the system more efficient, Western technology makes it easier to avoid such reforms. If one can imagine a Soviet economy that would be 100-percent automated and able to dispense with human labor altogether, such an economy would be entirely freed from the need to take the human factor into account. Of course, such an economy is not possible; but everything that contributes to the automation of Soviet production, that supplies it with that which the Stalinist system cannot provide, serves to solidify the despotic arrangement.

It is difficult to tell whether the democracies, constrained as they are by vested interests, public opinion, and political rivalries, are capable of sustaining an indirect, long-range policy, which requires the courage of quiet firmness and patience. Unquestionably, it is much easier to evoke a response from a democratic electorate with either calls to arms or promises of eternal peace. What can be said with confidence is that as long as the present, essentially Stalinist, system prevails in the Soviet Union, war will remain an ever-present danger which neither rearmament nor accommodation can entirely avert.

"Our policy should...respond to the Soviet challenge in ways that will protect our security, our interests, and our values, rather than try to force changes in the Soviet Union."

US Policy Should Modify Soviet Behavior

Marshall D. Shulman

The author of the following viewpoint, Marshall D. Shulman, discusses six questions about the Soviet Union and concludes that Soviet aggression is not caused by its communist system but rather by its pursuit of nation-state interests. The United States can compete with the Soviets at a lower level of danger by using the classic instruments of foreign policy, namely, balance of power strategy and a system of rewards and punishments. Dr. Shulman currently teaches international relations at Columbia University. He was formerly a special assistant to Secretary of State Dean Acheson and was a special adviser on Soviet affairs to Secretaries of State Cyrus Vance and Edmund Muskie.

As you read, consider the following questions:

1. What has replaced revolutionary ideology as the primary motivation for Soviet foreign policy, according to Dr. Shulman?
2. What difference does Dr. Shulman see between Soviet intervention in Angola and its invasion of Afghanistan?
3. Why does the author believe a policy that tries to change the Soviet system would be counterproductive?

Almost seven decades have passed since the revolution that led to the founding of the Soviet Union. For most of those years, relations between that country and our own have been animated by hostility, relieved only by brief intervals of abatement and passing hopes of some easement.

Each such interval, however, has been followed by an ever stronger expression of the conflict of power, beliefs, and purposes between the two nations. That conflict is now so deeply rooted and so intense that it evokes the destructive energies of both societies, weakening them and the fabric of the international system, threatening the possibility of catastrophe.

That hostility did not grow out of any natural antipathy between the peoples of the two countries, but with the passage of time each has come to be so persuaded of the malign intent of the other that it has become difficult to distinguish what is real and what is fancied in the perceptions each holds of the other.

Images and Caricatures

In the conduct of our foreign relations, Walter Lippmann observed, we operate on the basis of "pictures in our heads." The images of the Soviet Union held most widely in this country are stereotypes, and they warp our thinking in a number of ways. They are simple caricatures of a complex society. They are static and do not take into account the changes that have taken place, particularly since the death of Stalin. They are based on prevalent assumptions that do not bear critical examination. They misrepresent the ways in which the Soviet people react to our actions and to our words. They do not distinguish between atmosphere and substance. Finally, as oversimple images informing oversimple policy, they make it difficult for us to resolve the dilemma of whether we should try to change the Soviet system or try to improve our relations with it....

The problems presented by the Soviet Union are serious. But stereotypes do not provide us with an adequate basis for responding intelligently....Not everyone, and certainly not all of those who study Soviet behavior, will agree with what I regard as realistic or with my conclusions. But I believe that the time is overdue for us to address head-on some of the questions that underlie our present thinking about that country in order to contribute to a more rational discourse, beyond the level of partisan polemics.

In seeking to expand its power and influence around the world, are the Soviet Union's aspirations unlimited? Does it accept practical limitations on realizing its status as a superpower? Might it even become willing to live according to the norms of the international system?

Over the last sixty-seven years, we have witnessed the ascendancy of nation-state interests over revolutionary expectations and ideology as the primary motivation of Soviet foreign policy. It became apparent to the Soviet regime in its early years—and even

132

more so after World War II—that the proletariat of the West was showing no signs of the revolutionary potential that Lenin had ascribed to it. In response to this fact, Soviet policy was adapted to address the bourgeoisie of both the Western industrial societies and the developing world for the purpose of influencing governments to act in ways favorable to Soviet interests. Although revolutionary ideology is still part of the official rhetoric and although it is bolstered by a bureaucratic apparatus that has a stake in it, it has been modified in such a way as to put off to the indefinite future the realization of apocalyptic goals. Peaceful coexistence, which to Lenin meant a breathing spell, has become a long-term political strategy of competition by means short of war....

Soviet Ideology

Are Soviet leaders, then, guided by the ideology of Marxism-Leninism? If you were to ask them that question, their answer would be "Of course." None of them would say otherwise, and they seek sanction for every action, speech, article, or book by quoting from the storehouse of the writings of Marx, Engels, and, especially, Lenin.

Reckless Pressure

Because the Soviet regime is economically and ideologically stunted as well as diplomatically and militarily overextended and beleaguered, the leaders in the Kremlin can be expected to become increasingly intractable and bellicose. In other words, Soviet Russia is becoming dangerously threatening less because of its mounting than its failing strength. Some American officials and intellectuals recklessly urge that Russia be pressured on all fronts toward the end of unsettling the Soviet regime and breaking up the Eastern bloc. These groups need to be reminded that overspent major powers are not inclined to dig their own graves. Rather, they will resort to preventive war.

Arno J. Mayer, *Democracy*, January 1982.

Marxist-Leninist ideology, of course, is based on the prediction that capitalist systems are doomed to decay and collapse, that they will seek to stave off this outcome by imperialist aggression, but that, in the end, "socialism" as the Soviet Union defines it will prove more effective and will emerge as the universal form of social organization. In practice, Soviet theoreticians have had to take into account the fact that these predictions from the nineteenth and early twentieth centuries have not received much confirmation. The lesson has not been lost on Soviet theoreticians, who have reinterpreted some parts of the ideology while clinging to others, seeking legitimacy in hoped-for improvements in performance, or what Khrushchev called "goulash communism." In truth, there is as much variance in the Soviet interpretation of Marxism-Leninism today as there is in American Protestantism.

To say that Soviet political figures and writers claim consistency with Marxism-Leninism is not to say that their actions are derived from ideology. Certainly the historical analysis of capitalism influences the way the older Soviet political elites interpret events, but the sacred texts offer less and less guidance for making the practical decisions demanded by the complex society that the Soviet Union has become. With rare exceptions, even those youths who aspire to become members of the Soviet establishment master their catechism with cynicism (the sound of shuffling feet during lectures on "diamat"—dialectical materialism—is reminiscent of the noise during lectures for GIs on social hygiene), suggesting that when they take the levers of power into their hands, the ideas that will shape their thoughts and guide their actions will bear only the slightest resemblance to the ideas that inspired the Revolution.

Is the Soviet Union nevertheless inherently *expansionist?*

Some have argued that the answer to this question is yes. Should that be true, it would follow that in order to move Soviet behavior in the direction of greater restraint and responsibility it would be necessary to change the Soviet system in fundamental ways, and that this should be the primary objective of American policy. Those who take this position claim that it is only by external aggrandizement that the Soviet leadership can cement its power, claim legitimacy, and validate its view of history. Some even argue that there is a parallel between the Soviet Union and Nazi Germany, and that just as appeasement served to whet the Nazis' appetite, any accommodation with the Soviet Union can "only lead to disaster."

Nation-State Interests

The study of Soviet behavior, however, suggests that Soviet actions are more consistently explained by reference to the pursuit of nation-state interests than by some inner compulsion related to the structure of the system....

There is an expansive tendency in the Soviet Union's behavior, but it is impelled not by the nature of the system but by the sense that the country has grown into a great power. Moreover, it has been activated by opportunities that the Soviet Union itself has not created, and it has been guided by a careful calculus of risks and gains as well as by a capacity for prudence. This was illustrated most recently by the absence of an immediate Soviet reaction to the attack on Syria during the Israeli invasion of Lebanon.

The Nazi parallel is particularly misleading. Unlike the Nazis, Soviet leaders do not seek war. No one doubts that who has seen firsthand how fresh are the memories of the destruction and loss of life in World War II, or how universal is the appreciation of the consequences of nuclear war (much more universal than is the case in the United States). Soviet leaders have accepted and accommodated themselves to the practical constraints on their expansionist tendencies. They may hope that the future will bring more favorable opportunities, but faith in their historical inevitability has become ritualistic, and is advanced on national holidays with diminishing conviction.

Competitive Relationship

Even if the Soviet Union is not inherently expansionist, is it possible for us to maintain peaceful relations with it so long as it seeks to maximize its power and influence?

We have to accept the fact that the Soviet-American relationship is fundamentally competitive and is likely to remain so for the foreseeable future. What we must decide is whether it is in our interest to compete at a high level of confrontation or whether it is more sensible to manage the competition at lower levels of tension. If we seek to force the pace of military competition and to maximize pressure on the Soviet Union by cutting back diplomatic contacts, trade, and all forms of cooperation, the effect will be to increase the level of conflict and the risk of war and to push both societies toward greater, and destructive, militarization.

A Modest Policy

A modest policy of détente will satisfy neither the advocates of a more confrontationist policy nor the supporters of a more ambitious understanding with the Soviet Union. Whereas a modest policy of détente aims for no more than the normalization of the great rivalry, the more sweeping alternatives would move toward ending—by victory or accommodation—the conflict that has largely dominated the postwar world. Yet neither of these radical solutions has any reasonable prospect of being achieved.

This being so, we have no real alternative but to try to normalize the conflict, as much as possible. In this normalization lies the best hope of preserving an international order that has brought a remarkable measure of prosperity and stability to this nation and to the world.

Robert W. Tucker, *The New York Times Magazine*, December 9, 1984.

It is sometimes said in this country that the so-called détente of the early 1970s was a failure and a deception, and that it proved that the effort to moderate relations is bound not to work, leaving us at a disadvantage. But the principal reason why détente was not successful was that neither side fulfilled the two main requirements for reducing tensions. Those requirements are the management of the nuclear competition at lower and more stable levels and the codification of the terms of political competition in the Third World. On each side there were impediments to exercising the restraint that is essential to reducing the risk of war....

This period of international politics has been characterized by an extraordinary turbulence involving dramatic transformations in the industrialized nations, post-decolonization travails in the developing ones, and anarchy in the international system. Under the best of circumstances, it would have been remarkable if Soviet-American relations had not become roiled.

Has Soviet foreign policy, emboldened by what some analysts see as military supremacy, become more aggressive in the years since détente?

There is a two-part answer to the military question. Certainly the improvements in the Soviet Union's conventional capabilities, the increase in the firepower and mobility of its forces, and its greater logistical capabilities—demonstrated in the impressive airlift of matériel to Ethiopia—have made it possible to intervene where it might not have been able to a decade ago. But despite the expanded Soviet strategic nuclear arsenal, it is wrong to speak of supremacy, and there are no grounds for believing that the strategic balance influenced the Soviet decisions to act as it did in Angola, Ethiopia, or Afghanistan.

The lack of restraint shown by the Soviet Union in exacerbating local conflicts cannot be justified, but its interventions have represented a continuation of its longstanding policy of seeking to exploit opportunities, whatever their cause. The 1975 intervention in Angola, for example, was a response to the collapse of the Portuguese position in Africa....(In contrast, the Soviet invasion of Afghanistan was a response not to an opportunity but to a perceived threat; it can best be understood as a gross political and military miscalculation, reflecting Soviet paranoia about the security of its borders.)

Of course, even though these Soviet interventions were responses to opportunities rather than manifestations of a more aggressive policy, they are still a matter for concern. But it lies within our power to reduce such opportunities by understanding better what local factors generate upheavals and conflicts, and by responding to them more appropriately ourselves....

Soviet System

Is the Soviet system capable of change?

It is here that we come to a question that is absolutely fundamental to the way we think about the Soviet Union, and it is here that our stereotypes are most strikingly out of date. Since the Revolution, the Soviet Union has evolved from a predominantly peasant society to one that is largely urban and industrializing. Although the process of industrialization has moved forward unevenly, and although large parts of the country do not seem to have changed in the past 100 years, the spread of education and the growth of cadres of specialists have made for a much more complex society, in which controls have been increasingly internalized and "privatization" stubbornly protects pockets of autonomy from intrusion by the central authorities. Leaving the intellectuals aside, for most people the system works, since they compare their living standards not with those of other countries but with their own in the past....

The prevailing Western images of the Soviet elite, based on monolithic totalitarian models, tend to stereotype Soviet officialdom, leading some observers to conclude that the system is brittle and cannot change without risk of collapse. This obscures the spectrum of views to be found even within the party establishment, which encompasses not only those who are careerists and bureaucrats supreme but also those who might be called "within-system critics," those who, within the bounds of loyalty to the system, possess and sometimes express unorthodox views about modernization. Because the changes they favor may provoke resistance, in the short run their activities may reinforce or even increase the authority of the political police. Whether in the long run such changes will moderate the repressiveness of the Soviet system may depend in part on the international climate....

Factor of Change

There are, of course, other questions that we might wish to ask, but the issues we have already touched on point toward something that should be taken into account far more than has been the case: the factor of change. If instead of viewing the Soviet Union as a static system we view it as one in the midst of a historical trans-

---

Siege Mentality

Russians feel they have unassailable historical reasons for hypersensitivity about their homeland. Centuries of invasions and abuse by foreigners have persuaded them that protecting "the motherland" is rightly a paramount consideration....

For many years, an artificially exaggerated sense of siege has been a key tool for Soviet leaders seeking to maintain firm control over their huge and diverse country and empire. The presence, real or imagined, of hostile foreign dangers has been used to justify rigid internal controls.

Robert G. Kaiser, *The Minneapolis Tribune*, September 19, 1983.

---

formation, then the starting point for thinking through our own policies should be to ask ourselves how they are likely to affect the processes of change in the Soviet system, Soviet conduct in the world, and opportunities for peaceful relations between the two countries.

Our capacity to influence the nature of change in the Soviet

Union is limited. At the very least, however, we should exercise care lest our actions and words impair the prospects for changes we would like to see. It should be clear from past experience that if we are perceived to be bellicose, or if we declare our intent to undermine the Soviet order, we strengthen the backward elements in the Soviet political system.

It follows that our long-term policy should have an evolutionary purpose: it should be designed to encourage future generations of Soviet leaders to see that acting with restraint and enlarging the area of genuine cooperation between the United States and the Soviet Union serve their own self-interest. The main objective of our policy should therefore be to respond to the Soviet challenge in ways that will protect our security, our interests, and our values, rather than to try to force changes in the Soviet Union or to bring about changes in its foreign policy indirectly by seeking to undermine the Soviet system.

This does not mean that we are not interested in what happens inside the Soviet Union, nor that we should put aside our humanitarian concern about its repressive practices....But we should have learned from our recent experience that it is counterproductive for our government to make the human rights issue an instrument in a political offensive against the Soviet Union and to engage the prestige of the Soviet leadership by frontal, public ultimatums, as it did with the Jackson-Vanik amendment and in the tragic cases of Andrei Sakharov and Anatoly Shcharansky. We should also remember that although decreased international tension may in the short run inspire campaigns of ideological vigilance designed to control the spread of bourgeois ideas within the Soviet Union, increased levels of international tension reduce the restraints on the Soviet police apparatus and encourage greater pressures for retrogressive movement toward neo-Stalinism....

Managing the Competition

In the political competition between the United States and the Soviet Union, containment by military force is clearly an inadequate response. There may be occasions when we will need sufficient forces on the ground to prevent Soviet intervention, but this is only a negative capability. More important, we must learn to respond to the causes of the strains and instabilities that create opportunities for exploitation by the Soviet Union. For example, we have allowed our relations with our allies among the industrialized nations to become strained by economic tensions and by their growing lack of confidence in the sobriety and wisdom of our leadership. Yet it ought to be the very heart of our policy to maintain the closest possible ties with them. In the Third World, we must show greater awareness of the sources of instability than we have so far. If we are prepared to deal with the causes of revolutionary change, to address the issues of health, food, literacy, and equity with more understanding, we will be able to respond to these problems before all hope of peaceful resolution is lost and the only solution becomes military arbitration between equally unsavory extremes.

In our relations with the Soviet Union we should rely on incentives as well as on constraints. This means that we must sustain a reasonable level of trade and exchanges and encourage limited measures of cooperation. Holding out the prospect of widening ties as the Soviet Union shows its readiness to act responsibly is a token of our hope that the relationship can move to a less dangerous stage. This, indeed, is the link to our longer-term policy. We cannot assume that Soviet behavior will evolve in this way, but we can let future generations of Soviet leaders know that if they do move in this direction we are prepared to accept this more productive relationship.

Live with Constraints

At the center of our thinking should always be the concern that the protection of our security and our values depends not only on the sensible management of relations with the Soviet Union but on the condition of the international system itself, on those fragile restraints on the behavior of nations that have been created so slowly and painfully over the years. It must be strengthened against the anarchy and chaos that now threaten it. To do this we must seek not to preserve the status quo but to codify processes of nonviolent change. We must work toward placing constraints on the use of force to produce or to prevent change, and we must be willing, ourselves, to live within these constraints.

One more thing needs to be said. Essential to a *modus vivendi* are diplomatic communications with the Soviet Union, firm but not bellicose, conducted with civility and common sense—recently so uncommon in American politics.

Recognizing Statements That Are Provable

From various sources of information we are constantly confronted with statements and generalizations about social and moral problems. In order to think clearly about these problems, it is useful to be able to make a basic distinction between statements for which evidence can be found and other statements which cannot be verified or proved because evidence is not available or the issue is too controversial.

Readers should constantly be aware that magazines, newspapers and other sources often contain statements of controversial or questionable nature. The following activity is designed to allow experimentation with statements that are provable and those that are not.

Most of the following statements are taken from the viewpoints in this chapter. Consider each statement carefully. *Mark P for any statement you believe is provable. Mark U for any statement you feel is unprovable because of lack of evidence. Mark C for statements you think are too controversial to be proved to everyone's satisfaction.*

If you are doing this activity as a member of a class or group, compare your answers with those of other class or group members. Be able to defend your answers. You may discover that others will come to different conclusions than you. Listening to the reasons others present for their answers may give you valuable insights in recognizing statements that are provable.

If you are reading this book alone, ask others if they agree with your answers. You too will find this interaction very valuable.

> P = *provable*
> U = *unprovable*
> C = *too controversial*

1. The decision to seek détente in the early 1970s was an unwise exercise in wishful thinking.

2. The term "détente" has been in use since the early 1960s to connote a relaxation of tensions with the Soviet Union.

3. The strategy of détente succeeded remarkably well.

4. In 1979, the Soviet Union brutally invaded Afghanistan.

5. Containment has been a successful strategy.

6. Between 1945 and 1950, the Soviet Union imposed communism on all of Eastern and Central Europe.

7. The Soviet Union never stops regarding the United States as an adversary.

8. After World War II, Stalin violated the agreements signed in Teheran, Yalta, and Potsdam.

9. Both the theory and practice of communism are completely inhuman.

10. There will not be any nuclear war.

11. The Soviet Union has refused to furnish comprehensive data on its strategic systems.

12. The Soviet economy is self-sufficient.

13. COCOM was formed by NATO countries in 1949.

14. The Soviet economy has never been self-sufficient.

15. Present Soviet leaders are not guided by Marxist-Leninist ideology.

16. Democracy is under worldwide attack as it has never been before in its history.

17. Leadership changes more frequently in the United States than it does in the Soviet Union.

18. Marxist-Leninist ideology is based on the prediction that capitalist systems are doomed to decay and collapse.

19. Since the Revolution, the Soviet Union has evolved from a predominantly peasant society to one that is largely urban and industrializing.

20. Since 1921, the USSR has been importing materiel and know-how from the West to introduce new technology.

Bibliography

The following list of books, periodicals, and pamphlets deals with the subject matter of this chapter.

Conservative Digest	"Are Liberals Soft on Communism?" June 1984.
Barbara Epstein	"Unequal Giants: American Foreign Policy and the Soviet Union," *Socialist Review,* no. 72.
Raymond L. Garthoff	*Detente and Confrontation: American-Soviet Relations from Nixon to Reagan.* Washington, DC: Brookings, 1985.
Harry Gelman	"Rise and Fall of Détente," *Problems of Communism,* March/April 1985.
Robert Lasch	"War Fever: The Durable Myths of the Cold War Still Cast Their Spell," *The Progressive,* July 1980.
Patricia Marx	"Getting Along with the Russians," *Harper's,* January 1985.
Novosti Press Agency	*Soviet Foreign Policy: Questions and Answers.* Booklet available from the Soviet Embassy Information Department, 1706 Eighteenth St. NW, Washington, DC 20009. 1984.
Richard Pipes	*U.S.—Soviet Relations in the Era of Détente.* Boulder, CO: Westview Press, 1981.
Boris N. Ponomarev	*Communism in a Changing World.* New York, NY: Sphinx Press, Inc., 1983.
Ronald Reagan	"A Crusade for Freedom: Military Strength Is a Prerequisite for Peace," *Vital Speeches of the Day,* July 1, 1982.
Aleksandr Solzhenitsyn	"Communism at the End of the Brezhnev Era," *National Review,* January 21, 1983.
Strobe Talbott	"Communism: The Specter and the Struggle," *Time,* January 4, 1982.
Robert W. Tucker	"Toward a New Détente," *The New York Times Magazine,* December 9, 1984.
Aaron Wildavsky	*Beyond Containment: Alternative American Policies Toward the Soviet Union.* San Francisco, CA: Institute for Contemporary Studies, 1983.

Communism in the Third World: Success or Failure?

Introduction

The viewpoints in this final chapter focus on two important issues for developing nations. The first four viewpoints consider which economic system—communism or capitalism—better helps Third World nations develop their economies. The last four viewpoints concentrate on the question of independence for developing nations from the political and economic influence of both the West and the Soviet Union.

The emergence of Third World communism complicates the question of which economic system is best for promoting economic development. Most Marxist Third World countries have adapted Marxism in some way in hopes of making it work better for their particular needs. The authors in this chapter debate whether these adaptive Marxist systems are actually communist and whether they have improved their economies.

Third World countries' desires for independence from Western influence is traceable to the long period of colonization they experienced. Some Third World specialists question the amount of independence developing nations have since they still depend on Western markets and trade even though they are no longer colonies.

Many of these specialists emphasize the distrust toward Western nations still felt by the ex-colonies. But the Soviet Union's actions in the Third World have raised suspicion as well, a subject the last two viewpoints discuss. They consider whether Communist countries in the Third World are truly independent or are victims of Soviet imperialism.

"The Cuban development strategy...has been committed to satisfy the basic needs of the population as a first priority."

Communism Has Helped Cuba

Claes Brundenius

A key issue in the debate about economic systems is the choice between economic growth and economic fairness. Communists argue that although capitalism may promote growth, it does not distribute wealth fairly and profits stay in the hands of the rich. Since communism distributes wealth, they say, it is a fairer system. In the following viewpoint, Claes Brundenius, an economist at the University of Lund in Sweden, argues that since its Communist revolution in 1959 Cuba has more equitably distributed wealth than other Third World nations. This viewpoint is taken from a paper he presented to the Association of Third World Economists.

As you read, consider the following questions:

1. In what ways has education reduced Cuba's unemployment, according to the author?
2. Name three things Mr. Brundenius cites which benefited rural Cuba.
3. According to the author, how does Brazil's development strategy differ from that of Cuba?

It is today widely recognized that revolutionary Cuba has done comparatively well in solving the most urgent problems of poverty inherited from the past. It has also been assumed that the Cuban performance has been associated with a radical redistribution of income although quantitative evidence has been lacking. What is perhaps not so universally known is the boom of the Cuban economy during the first half of the 1970s with growth rates paralleling those of the Brazilian "miracle" which took place about the same time. Economic growth in the post-revolutionary period (1959-1979) compares very favourably with the pre-revolutionary era as will be shown in this paper. What is true is that economic growth was very sluggish in the 1960s and was even negative during some bad years in the middle of the decade, but it is argued that this failure to meet growth targets was less a result of incompatibility between growth and equity goals than of gross inefficiencies of an overcentralized and bureaucratic planning system....

Reducing Unemployment

The perhaps most serious problem haunting many under-developed countries, not least in Latin America, is that of high rates of open unemployment coupled with perhaps half of the population of working age being underemployed in subsistence agriculture and in the service sector in exploding cities....On the eve of the revolution over half of the rural labour force of 900,000 workers was employed in the cane fields and during the "dead season" it has been estimated that more than 400,000 workers were unemployed, the majority of them being sugar workers. These numbers represented about 20% of the total labour force but even during the *zafra* (November-April) open unemployment was as high as 9-11%.

Despite determined efforts by the government to tackle the problems of those deprived of adequate work, open unemployment was as high as 9% as late as 1962. But then, during the following six years, the unemployment rate went down to 4.3% thanks to mass mobilization, the expansion of the educational system, making young people stay longer at school, and not least, the effects of massive emigration during especially the first five years of the revolution. By 1970—the year of the 10 million *zafra*—the unemployment rate was as low as 1.3%....

Women have always constituted a large labour reserve in Cuba, as in most other parts of Latin America, but they have seldom been motivated to join the labour force. This is partly due to attitudes, partly it is a reflection of already high unemployment and underemployment rates. After the revolution considerable efforts have gone into changing these attitudes and with the expansion of the educational system it has been natural for girls to look for jobs after leaving school. When this new generation of girls, with at least six years of primary education, started leaving school at the beginning of the 1970s, female participation rates also started increasing dramatically. These new entries into the labour force came at a time when the Cuban economy was experiencing an unprecedented boom period, at the peak of which (1972-1976) the female labour force increased by some 226,000, or by almost 50%, explaining over 75% of the new entries into the work force during that period....

A New Mentality

After years of human exploitation by foreigners, Cuba has undergone a social revolution which is setting a pattern for much of the present world....

There is more than economic development involved in the remarkable story of modern Cuba. There, and in other socialist nations, there is a new mentality emerging. Everyone is involved in planning, harvesting or developing the society and making it succeed. Work is a dignified, desirable activity....As a result of the Cuban revolution, it is my observation that the average person in Cuba has the highest standard of living of any nation in Central America.

Edward Lamb, *The Churchman*, November 1984.

To a certain extent the supply of labour has been offset by a very progressive retirement law, applicable to women from the age of 55 and for men over 60 years of age. It is no exaggeration to claim that Cuba has the most advanced social security system in Latin America covering practically 100% of the population. The corresponding coverage is in Brazil 32%, in Chile 69.5% (before Pinochet), in Mexico 25%, and in Peru 36%. On the other hand, such an advanced social security system is becoming increasingly costly and makes the pressure against resources and low productivity even more obvious....

Improved Health Care

The Cuban health record is impressive, not least considering that about one-third of all doctors left the country during the first three years after the revolution. Medical services also suffered during the first decade when the Ministry of Education and the universities, in order to compensate this brain drain, reduced the requirements for medical professions.

The health situation also deteriorated in these years. Thus, the infant mortality rate went up from 34.9 to 46.7 per thousand in 1969 but has then gradually fallen and was in 1978 as low as 22.3, one of the lowest rates recorded in the Third World. During the second decade many diseases have been completely eradicated in Cuba (malaria and polio-myelitis), and mortality rates sharply reduced as in the cases of tuberculosis, diphtheria and intestinal parasitism. This is no doubt the result of the rapid expansion of medical facilities in the 1970s, especially as regards number of physicians, dentists and nurses. The success is particularly due to the extension of medical services to the *rural areas*. Medical treatment is totally free and newly graduated doctors have to do obligatory service for at least two years in the countryside. At the same time that the administration of health has been centralized, its execution has been very much decentralized. Medical care has been provided free side-by-side with the active mobilization of the population to attain massive immunization, blood donations, the clearing of garbage dumps and similar activities, in most cases organized by the numerous Committees for the Defence of the Revolution.

Literacy Campaign

The educational expansion is perhaps the most spectacular accomplishment of the Cuban revolution. In the 1960s the stress was laid on raising the minimum levels of education of the population and one of the first achievements was the historic literacy campaign in 1961 when some 200,000 Cubans were mobilized under the slogan "Let those who know more teach those who know less." In this way, in less than one year the illiteracy rate went down from 23.6% for Cubans aged over 10 (and in the countryside the figure was double that rate) to 3.9%, an accomplishment later corroborated by UNESCO and described as probably unequalled in the history of education. An important aspect of this campaign was the fact that making people literate was not seen as an end in itself but rather a means for the integration of these earlier marginalized sectors of the population into the new society. When the literacy campaign ended, an ambitious programme to elevate the educational levels of people at large was launched, and primary and secondary schooling was offered in farms, factories, offices and night schools....

The most spectacular expansion of education did not, however, take place in the 1960s but in the 1970s, the reason being the explosion, to say the least, of secondary education—enrollments by the end of the 1970s were more than ten times higher than before the revolution. In 1979 compulsory schooling embraced no less than 92% of all children between 6-16 years old, and more than one-third of the total population was attending some type of school....

Income Redistribution

Although little quantitative information has been supplied by the Cuban government to support the claim that a radical redistribution of incomes and assets has taken place in the country after the revolution, few observers of the Cuban revolution seem to doubt it. As a matter of fact, Dudley Seers considers that "the degree of equality in Cuba is now probably unique," and Robert Bernado even argues that Cuba "is the first [country] to institutionalize the communist or egalitarian rule of production and distribution." Although those claims may be somewhat exaggerated they nevertheless reflect the large number of redistributive reforms and laws enacted after the revolution, especially during the first ten years.

Social Progress

For the first time, Cubans are masters of their own country. Nobody can belittle them for being black or discriminate against them for being women. Their social status is not determined by their income. To find a bed in a hospital in case of illness, or a job, they no longer have to humiliate themselves if they are men or prostitute themselves if they are women, as used to be the case. Our economy has grown at an approximate annual average rate of 4.7 percent over 25 years, one of the highest in the continent despite the U.S. blockade and, in Latin America, we are the second country in food consumption per capita. In the fields of health, education, culture and sports, we rank first among Third World countries and better than many industrialized countries. It would surprise you if I tell you that in proportion to the total populations, there are more illiterates and semi-illiterates in the United States than in Cuba.

Fidel Castro, *Newsweek*, January 9, 1984.

The most important reform was the Agrarian Reform Law of May 1959. Its provisions can be summarized as follows:
1. a maximum limit of 400 hectares on land ownership,
2. the transfer of land to those who farm it but do not own it,
3. The establishment of peoples' farms and sugar cooperatives in place of the large expropriated sugar estates,
4. the nationalization of 40% of all rural property,
5. compensation to owners of expropriated land in the form of Agrarian Bonds, redeemable within a period of 20 years and with a 4½% interest rate.

The Agrarian Reform had, of course, a tremendous effect on income distribution in the rural areas, not only because the large *latifundistas* were deprived of much of their land but also because the small farmer could get land very cheap. The first 27 hectares of land were given to the small farmer (*campesino*) free, with the right to purchase a further 40 hectares. It has been estimated that some 100,000 *campesinos* benefited from this reform. In October 1963, a second and final Agrarian Reform Law was passed, limiting the area of land which could be owned privately to 66 hectares.

Benefits to the Poor
In the urban sector the most effective redistributive reform was the Rent Law of March 1959, implying reductions of 50% in the

rents of all who paid less than 100 pesos per month and of 30 or 40% for tenants in the higher brackets. The wealthy were shocked by this drastic measure denounced as virtual confiscation of their private property, and considered to be Castro's first "betrayal" to the bourgeois supporters of the revolution. But there were many other reforms or laws that meant *de facto* redistribution of income and wealth. Thus, for instance, the minimum salary was raised, prices of medicine, electricity and gas were lowered, gambling and prostitution were suppressed, back payments of salaries and retirement pensions of people fired during the Batista regime were honoured, and the establishment of "peoples' stores" (especially in the rural areas) guaranteed the supply of basic goods at low prices.

The redistribution of income that took place during the first two years was indeed impressive. Exactly how much was redistributed is not known, but it has been calculated that more than 500 million pesos annually, or 20% of the average national income in the period 1959-1960, was redistributed in those years....

An important redistribution of income took place just after the revolution, benefiting principally the poorest 40% of the population, although the middle deciles also appear to have gained in the process. Between 1962 and 1973 a further redistribution of income took place but at a much slower pace than before....

Although not unique in the world, the income redistribution for the benefit of the poor that has taken place in Cuba after 1959 is by all means unique in Latin America. In most of the Latin American countries the income share of the poorest 40% of the population seldom reaches 10%, and in many countries the share has even been decreasing during the last two decades. In the case of Brazil, the poorest 40% received only 7.9% of the income in 1976, which should be compared with 10.1% in 1970, and 11.5% in 1960. In Peru the trend has been the same. While the two first quintiles in 1961 got 10% of the income, this share had by 1972 decreased to 8%, and for the lowest quintile the situation has aggravated even more drastically, from 3.0% to 1.4%.

Alternative Development Strategies

Brazil and Peru are interesting cases to compare since both countries have, rightly or wrongly, been associated with alternative development strategies. Brazil has been the most pronounced advocate of the theory that a growth-oriented strategy will in the long run also benefit the poor, and that "the cake has to grow before it can be eaten." Peru is interesting because the military government, which came into power in 1968, promised to redistribute both assets and income through radical measures such as land reform, nationalizations of basic industries, and workers' participation in profits and management, but all measures were to be carried out in accordance with a genuine Peruvian "model" that would be "neither reformed capitalism nor authoritarian communism."...

150

There seem to have been some "trickle down" benefits, that is crumbs for the poor, from the rapid economic growth experienced in Brazil, especially during the so-called economic miracle (1967-1974). In spite of getting *relatively* lower shares of income it seems that even the poorest 20% of the population have increased their real incomes somewhat, although they are still far below the subsistence level. The Peruvian case is much worse than the Brazilian one. Between 1961 and 1972 the situation for the very poor—the bottom 20%—has dramatically deteriorated, not only in relative terms but also *absolutely*, with at least 20% of the population living below the "poverty line" in 1972. And 1972 was a boom year before recession started to cripple the Peruvian economy some years later. Although no statistics on income distribution are available for later years, it is quite clear that the real income level of the poor cannot possibly have ameliorated since 1972.

Concluding, one might argue that the Cuban experience of income redistribution shows that the strategies, explicit or implicit, that have been pursued have managed to raise considerably the income situation for the large majority of the population, and that this shift in income distribution compares favourably in relation to both Brazil and Peru. In Brazil, the government now openly

---

Declaration of Independence

In their heart of hearts, Latin Americans across the political map, from Shining Path to capitalist road, know that Fidel Castro did it, defended it and made it work, at least as well as could be expected under the circumstances. Cuba's declaration of independence from North American power did not bring the country economic abundance, social harmony or national self-sufficiency, but it created an absolutely necessary condition for development according to the needs and means of Cuba's people.

Andrew Kopkind, *The Nation*, August 17/24, 1985.

---

recognizes that "growth may not solve the problem of adequate distribution of income, if left to the mere evolution of market factors," and in Peru the military government recently had to hand back the presidential palace to the very man it twelve years earlier had evicted from power—a symbolic act illustrating the total collapse of the once celebrated "Peruvian model."

Satisfying Basic Needs

It has sometimes been argued by critics of basic needs oriented strategies that such an approach is bound to inhibit growth since it is basically consumption oriented. Cuba has been used as a case in point in view of the sluggish growth rates recorded in the 1960s. Dudley Seers, however, finds the issue to be misleading and says that "the important question to pose about a country's performance is not, how much did the nation's income grow? But rather, whose income grew?"...

Cuban Development Strategy

What is perhaps the most impressive feat of the Cuban development strategy is that it has been committed to satisfy the basic needs of the population as a first priority in spite of mounting economic problems during the latter part of the 1970s.

"At the root of Cuba's debt rescheduling problems are its Soviet-style command economy, high interest rates..., and fallen sugar prices."

Communism Has Hurt Cuba

Wilson P. Dizard III

Cuba's foreign debt problem has been exacerbated by the failure of its communist economy to grow, according to the author of the following viewpoint, Wilson P. Dizard III. Mr. Dizard is a Research Associate with the Cuban American National Foundation in Washington, DC. He argues that communism in Cuba has not only failed to provide growth, it has also been unfair to the masses who suffer when economic cutbacks have to be made.

As you read, consider the following questions:

1. According to Mr. Dizard, how has Cuba spent much of the foreign loan money it has received?
2. What evidence does the author give to support his contention that Cuban workers are dissatisfied?
3. How has the US embargo hurt Cuba, according to the author?

Wilson P. Dizard, "Cuba in the Red," is excerpted from an article of the same title which appeared in *Worldview*, March 1983, Vol. 26, No. 3. Reprinted by permission of the Council on Religion and International Affairs.

[H]as not Batista jeopardized the credit of the country for 30 years? Has not the public debt increased to more than 800 million pesos? Is there not a deficit of more than 100 million? Are not the monetary reserves of the nation pledged to foreign banks in a desperate search for money? Were not 350 million pesos of the most recent loan wasted on the purchase of jet planes and things of that nature, without plan or program, for no other reason than personal whim? Can one play in this manner with the destiny of a nation? Did anyone authorize him to undertake these insane credit ventures? Did he consult the people in any way?...It is for us more than anyone else to be concerned because we and future generations will have to pay the terrible consequences of that corrupt and unchecked policy.

Fidel Castro, Manifesto No. 1 to the People of Cuba, August 8, 1955.

In the spring of 1982 the Cuban American National Foundation in Washington, D.C., published a report that predicted that Havana's hard currency debt to Western banks and governments was "unmanageably large and headed toward a crisis." On August 31, 1982, the Banco Nacional de Cuba (BNC) announced its intention to reschedule approximately half of its roughly $3 billion of hard currency debt. In early January, 1983, the Cuban Government suspended payments on the principal of that debt.

Cuba's Western Debt

Two key issues discussed in the 1982 foundation report were the possibility of Soviet backing for Cuba in its debt difficulties and the uses to which the Castro regime has put the funds raised from Western banks and governments. Because some of the credits Havana had received from Western banks were not linked to any particular project, they were available for use in Cuba's Soviet-inspired military adventures in Latin America, Africa, the Middle East, and Asia. If the borrowed funds were not used directly to fund these operations, they were certainly available to replace assets that had been diverted to these military endeavors.

When Cuban government officials visited Tokyo to outline their proposal for rescheduling the debt to Japanese banks, speculation on the first of the issues was put to rest. They surprised Japanese bankers by indicating that the Soviet Union would *not* serve as a lender of last resort for the Castro regime. Some of the BNC's foreign creditors remained unconvinced, however, and at a meeting of its creditors held in Paris in November, 1982, the delegate from the United Kingdom pointedly referred to the possibility that the Soviet Union could lend Cuba the hard currency it needs.

In the same month a high-level delegation of European and Japanese officials representing the treasury ministries of nations that have extended credit to the Castro government met in Havana to begin discussion on the rescheduling of Cuba's debt. Among the nations affected are France, Japan, Germany, Spain, Italy, Argentina, Canada, Mexico, and several in the Arab world. (Cuba's debt consists of both trade credits extended by government agencies and loans from private banks. Negotiations with the government agencies will set the pattern for subsequent talks with international banks.)

The rescheduling itself came as no surprise to international banking circles, which long had been aware of the vulnerability of the Cuban economy. Bankers in Western Europe, Canada, and Japan who had arranged loans for Cuba were, however, taken aback by the terms now being sought. The BNC, its motives variously described as "arrogance" and "naiveté," was demanding a ten-year rescheduling period to be initiated by a three-year grace period, during which the payment on medium and long-term debt principal would be suspended. Havana rested this proposal on several conditions intended to protect Cuba's short-term loan arrangements, which were not being rescheduled. The Banco Nacional de Cuba asserted that Cuba is "a special case" and deserves preferential treatment from its creditors. According to government authorities, "Cuba is a country under aggression and therefore requires conditions that mitigate the consequences of aggression."

The BNC's demand for "special treatment" was met with coolness. As the *Financial Times* of London put it: "Cuba can make

Reprinted with permission: Tribune Media Services.

no claim for privileged treatment by the West on either political or economic grounds." To the contrary, "It is obvious that Western banks need not rush to the help of a government whose economic sectarianism and whose willingness to sacrifice its own people's living standards to foreign campaigns has left its finances in a perilous state."

The Castro government's economic leaders spearheaded their rescheduling campaign by releasing a sixty-seven page "Economic Report," a curious document consisting chiefly of excuses and rationalizations for Havana's economic crisis. Of the relatively few statistics provided, many are transparent fabrications.

The thrust of the report was to assign blame for the negative aspects of the Cuban economy to the U.S. or the pre-1959 governments. For example, a series of statistics purport to show that the Castro regime inherited a chronic trade deficit. In fact, Cuba ran a consistent trade surplus during the 1950s, with the exception of 1958, when trade was disrupted by guerrilla activities. Similarly, the report states that the infant mortality rate in the period immediately preceding the 1959 revolution was 60 per thousand live births. This conflicts with reports by the Pan American Union and the World Bank, which put the figure in the range of 36 to 38 per thousand. The BNC asserts that in 1959 a Cuban's life expectancy was 53 years, while the World Bank offers the figure in 1960 as 64 years.

Labor Problems

While the BNC's intent in publishing these social data was to propound the official ideology, which assigns all positive developments in Cuba to the successes of the present regime, their publication tended to cast doubt on the veracity of the financial statistics presented in the report, thereby undermining the regime's credibility among its creditors. *Not* addressed in the Economic Report is one of the great imponderables of Cuba's economic future: the day in 1986, fast approaching, when Cuba must begin repaying its debt to the Soviet Union, estimated at nearly $7 billion.

At the root of Cuba's debt rescheduling problems are its Soviet-style command economy, high interest rates around the world, and fallen sugar prices. These factors are compounded, in turn, by low worker morale, leading to stagnant productivity and high rates of absenteeism. Despite efforts to counteract these trends by mobilizing large segments of the population for "voluntary" work, the prevailing impression among Cuban workers is that personal economic advancement is unlikely under the current system, hence the pressure to emigrate represented by the Mariel exodus of 1980. Additional evidence of worker disaffection has been provided even in the speeches of high Cuban government officials, including General Raul Castro Ruz, Fidel Castro's brother and the number two man in the government. In a speech in December,

1979, General Castro criticized widespread absenteeism, shirking, falsification of statistics, and other lapses of labor discipline. In recent years the regime has attempted to counteract these practices with coercion in the form of the massive price increases instituted in December of 1981 and through incentives in the form of cars, appliances, and vacations....

First Option

First option: sugar. Cuba's excessive reliance on sugar ties the economy's convertible currency prospects to the fluctuations of an essentially uncontrollable commodity price. While the bulk of Cuba's sugar crop is sold to the Soviet Union at artificially high prices under the so-called "slippery price system" (which also provides for sales of oil to Cuba by the Soviet Union at artificially low prices), these transactions do not generate the hard currency needed for repayment of Western debts. It should be mentioned in this connection that trade with the Soviet Union, despite these concessionary terms, has in recent years generated an imbalance in favor of the USSR. The price of Cuban exports to the Soviet Union were at one stage indexed to the expense of Cuban imports from that country so that trade would balance automatically. However, this arrangement has changed in recent years to Cuba's disadvantage: In 1979, Cuba had a $186 million trade deficit in bilateral trade with the Soviets, which increased to $670 million in 1980.

Domestic Stagnation

Although Soviet economic aid alone is now equivalent to more than one-quarter of Cuba's gross national product, per capita income in Cuba has been stagnant and is falling steadily relative to much of Latin America. Even the much-acclaimed initial improvements in social and health services have lost luster with the passage of time. Infant mortality and life expectancy already met high standards in 1959; under Castro, they have improved less than in many other developing countries. For almost a quarter century, social mobility has been capped by the permanence of a self-perpetuating elite more rigid than any traditional oligarchy.

Thomas O. Enders, in a speech before the House Foreign Affairs Committee, December 14, 1982.

Diversification of the economy was one of the original goals of the 26th of July Movement, Castro's organization in the early days of the Revolution. As early as August, 1955, in the "Manifesto No. 1 to the Cuban People," Castro called for "immediate industrialization of the country by means of a vast plan made and promoted by the state." These efforts have not met with success, and

Cuba is now more dependent on sugar than it was before the Revolution. Nor has this activity itself been fully industrialized, since the bulk of the sugar exported to the Soviet Union is in raw form for processing there.

Second Option

Second option: tobacco, citrus, and nickel. The disappointing outlook for sugar raises the question of Cuba's other export industries. The tobacco industry is in a period of recovery from the blue-mold disease that crippled the crop in 1979 and 1980. Though Cuba is a net exporter of tobacco, it has been importing some of the leaf recently to build up inventories depleted by the blight. A good crop was harvested in 1982, but the damage to stored tobacco caused by hurricane "Alberto" held down the recovery of tobacco exports. Tobacco is Cuba's most famous export after sugar, but its proportion of total exports is less than 5 per cent in most years.

Production Lags

Citrus production continues to lag behind planned goals. Last year's output of 160,000-170,000 tons fell far short of the projected 270,000 tons. Due to the low quality of the product, it is unsuitable for the world market and so is shipped to CMEA (Soviet bloc) countries.

Prospects for increased nickle production, another export, are not bright. Cuba's Soviet and CMEA allies have promised to build two new plants to raise production to a level of 100,000 tons annually (compared with the current output of approximately 40,000 tons), but disagreements over plant design have delayed completion of these projects until 1985 at the earliest. Meanwhile, nickel processing will continue at two confiscated U.S. plants. These obsolete facilities date from the era of low oil prices and so consume far more oil than do the modern plants in countries competing with Cuba.

The nickel industry worldwide is in the grips of a recession that has idled most of the industry's capacity and led to the buildup of large inventories, as in the case of sugar. Top U.S. nickel experts are skeptical of the Cuban Government's ability to expand production according to its goals. They point out that Cuba's laterite ore requires much more energy-intensive processing than do sulphide ores from Canada and other exporters. As with other goods, Cuban nickel exports are subject to the U.S. embargo, so the Cuban Government at times has attempted to "launder" them through France and the Soviet Union—only to be caught.

Third Option

Third option: tourism. Tourism is Cuba's most obvious potential resource: It is abundantly endowed with the natural resources of topography, climate, and the sport fishing available in coastal waters. And tourism has the advantage of being labor-intensive and nonpolluting.

Before 1959 the island attracted 300,000 tourists each year, principally from the United States, a trade known as "the second sugar harvest." Tourism development is, in fact, one of the Castro regime's top priorities. Cuban authorities hoped to attract 200,000 visitors in 1982; however, in 1981 the industry earned only $80 million in hard currency. By contrast, Jamaica's tourism revenue was $263 million that year. Again, politics was the stumbling block: The Reagan administration has effectively curtailed American tourism in Cuba, charging Castro's continuing military adventurism....

Fourth Option

Fourth option: domestic austerity. Havana's rescheduling is also complicated by the fact that Cuba is not a member of the International Monetary Fund, which usually participates in these negotiations and acts as a referee to ensure implementation of the austerity measures needed to put the debtor's financial house in order. Anticipating the bankers' demand for fiscal responsibility, the BNC's Economic Report offered a seven-point program, which included:

- restriction on economic growth so as to keep hard currency imports at a minimum;
- concentration on CMEA-supported investment projects;
- priority attention to integration with CMEA countries;
- use of increased export revenue or new credits to build up monetary reserves;

Dependency

The Cuban economy is highly dependent on the Soviet Union and Eastern Europe, which account for some 85-90 per cent of its trade....Cuba remains a single-crop economy that exports a few raw materials to the Soviet Union and buys from it most of its intermediate and capital goods. The island has been unable to accumulate enough capital from domestic resources, has made little progress in expanding the capital goods sector, and has been incapable of self-sustained economic growth.

Irving Louis Horowitz, *Worldview*, December 1983.

- a search for joint ventures with Western companies in tourism, shipping of exports, and service industries under the new foreign investment law;
- promotion of sales to foreign countries of civil engineering services and technical knowhow;
- efforts to stabilize world sugar prices, notably by discouraging subsidized beet-sugar exports by the European Economic Community.

The brunt of the austerity measures ("restriction of economic growth so as to keep hard currency imports at a minimum") is unlikely to fall on the Party, the military, or government elites, leaving the mass population to bear the burden.

Fifth Option

Fifth option: opening toward the U.S. Before the 1959 Revolution the U.S. accounted for 75 per cent of Cuba's exports and 65 per cent of its imports. At least one official in Havana has expressed the hope as quoted in *The Economist [in June 1982]...* that "the United States could still be our most important economic partner." However, U.S. officials maintain that improved economic relations hinge on changes in Castro's aggressive promotion of subversion in Africa and Latin America and are perhaps most deeply concerned about Cuban support of terrorism in Puerto Rico. Last December, Thomas O. Enders, assistant secretary of state for inter-American Affairs, speaking before the House Subcommittee on Inter-American Affairs, noted that "in very high-level secret talks, our negotiators explored a series of steps with the eventual goal of removing the embargo and full diplomatic relations, in return for curbs on Cuban activities in Puerto Rico and a gradual withdrawal of more than 20,000 Cuban troops from Angola."...

As Cuba struggles to deal with its current credit problems, Fidel Castro's prerevolutionary indictment of the Batista government echoes with an ironic ring:

> Are not the monetary reserves of the nation pledged to foreign banks in a desperate search for money?...Can one play in this manner with the destiny of a nation? Did anyone authorize him to undertake these insane credit ventures? Did he consult the people in any way?

"What began as minor repair of the PRC's socialist economic system...has developed...into a serious attempt to restructure China's Soviet-type command economy."

China Is Repudiating Communism

Jan S. Prybyla

Since the 1975 death of Mao Zedong, who led China's Communist revolution in 1949, observers have speculated on how China will change with new leadership. Western observers continue to argue over the meaning and extent of the reforms Chinese leader Deng Xiaoping has introduced. Jan S. Prybyla, the author of the following viewpoint, argues that because of communism's failure, China will institute capitalist measures in an effort to revive and develop its economy. Mr. Prybyla teaches at Pennsylvania State University and has written several articles about China.

As you read, consider the following questions:

1. What factor led some Chinese economists to conclude the communist system itself, not just the way China had applied it, is to blame for China's economic problems, according to Mr. Prybyla?
2. According to the author, how has China reformed its agricultural system, and why have the reforms succeeded?

Jan S. Prybyla, "China's New Economic Strategy: Defining the US Role," *Asian Studies Center Backgrounder*, April 8, 1985. Reprinted with permission.

In a remarkable speech this January, Communist Party Chief Hu Yaobang admitted that the government of the People's Republic of China (PRC) had "wasted 20 years" because of "radical leftist nonsense" associated with the policies of Mao Zedong and the Gang of Four. Hu attributed China's turmoil during the period of the Great Leap Forward through the Cultural Revolution (1958-1976) to the Party's trying to solve economic problems with radical slogans such as "better to have socialist weeds than capitalist seedlings."

Hu's candid public remarks confirmed officially what all Chinese certainly have known for years (and what foreign boosters of Mao's China refused to admit)—that the Chinese communist economy was a shambles. Shortly after Mao's death, horror stories about the PRC economy began pouring out of Beijing. The problems, documented in a number of studies by Chinese economists and widely advertised by post-Mao politicians, stemmed primarily from the quality of economic performance rather than of production, although quantity per capita was also exceptionally low. By the time Deng Xiaoping asserted his authority in 1978, the PRC economy was "like a cancer-stricken patient in urgent need of therapy." Three matters badly needed attention: (1) the ills plaguing the economy had to be identified; (2) the causes of those ills had to be diagnosed; and (3) remedies had to be prescribed and applied....

Intense Internal Debate

The Chinese found the causes more difficult to recognize, because socialist economic theory offered few tools to analyze structural deficiencies within a state-planned system. By 1979, however, some Chinese economists were cautiously blaming the economic system itself and urging reform instead of mere adjustment.

The remedies prescribed and applied have been subject to intense internal debate within the PRC. Essentially, the argument has raged between those advocating policy adjustments within the state-planned system and those arguing for reform of the economic system. Although the initial remedies were in the form of adjustments, later policies have reflected some structural changes in the system.

The far-reaching nature of these structural changes made a strong conservative backlash inevitable. Too many communist cadres found their privileged positions eroded. And too many tenets of Party doctrine were cast aside in the march toward economic modernization. As the reforms proceed, opposition is likely to mount....

Ills of the PRC Economy

The PRC's major economic ills have been reflected in a number of symptoms. Among them:

1. Massive misallocations of resources. This resulted in: shortages of some goods and services while others were in surplus; high inventory levels; and long construction cycles that tied down scarce fixed capital.

2. Poor quality of inputs. While the rate of investment rose steadily over the years, the effectiveness of this investment steadily declined. There was, in other words, growth without productivity gains. Between 1952 and 1977, agricultural productivity declined significantly. Industrial productivity began to fall in the early 1970s. Raw materials utilization rates were among the highest in the world, with the pampered heavy industry being the worst offender.

3. Poor quality of outputs. Producer and consumer goods and services have been of low quality.

4. Structural imbalance. Heavy industry grew very fast compared with light (consumer goods) industry, transportation, and agriculture. Within heavy industry, machinery output grew faster than the growth of the energy needed to run the machines. As a result, much industrial capacity was idle over extended periods of time.

Thriving Small Businesses

Societies that have made the most spectacular progress in the shortest period of time are...where people have been allowed to create, compete, and build, where they've been permitted to think for themselves, make economic decisions, and benefit from their own risks....

Well, today in China, the reality of more small enterprises doing a thriving business, more families profiting from their own hard work and the bigger harvests they produce, and the more investment in science and technology points to more opportunity for all.

Ronald Reagan, in a speech in Beijing, China, April 27, 1984.

5. Unpredictability. The economy was subject to violent, unpredictable swings. The biggest of these, the post-Great Leap Forward depression (1960-1962), brought in its train an absolute drop in population of 13 million.

6. Widespread underemployment. This plagued both agriculture and industry.

Shortages

7. Excessive price subsidies. Over 30 percent of essential goods, especially foods produced by inefficient agricultural practices, were subsidized, imposing a heavy drain on the state budget. In 1979-1981, subsidies absorbed close to one-third of government budgetary revenues. Subsidies also artificially suppressed inflation. Along with the permanent shortage of goods, these created a permanent sellers' market for most goods and services.

8. Sluggish innovation and diffusion of modern technology. Between 1957 and 1978, China's technological lag behind the industrialized countries seriously widened. The corps of scientists, engineers, technicians, managers, and other professional experts was meager even by the standards of developing countries.

9. Low per capita income. In 1979, per capita gross national product (GNP) was $253, in the same range as that of Kenya or Sudan. One-third of the rural production teams (the basic farming unit at that time) had a yearly per capita net income of less than $65. Officially designated basic subsistence in rural areas required an annual per capita income of $75. This meant that, after more than two decades of rural collectivization, as many as 300 million Chinese existed below the subsistence level. In 1978, 80 percent of peasant expenditures went for food and clothing—almost no change since 1952. Between 1962 and 1980 the annual rate of growth of foodgrains per capita was 0.4 percent. Between 1963 and 1978, average industrial wages fell by at least 20 percent in real terms. There had been no general increase in urban money wages for 20 years, while prices of nonstaple commodities had mounted substantially.

Causes of the Problems

Identifying causes for the poor condition of the PRC economy proved difficult for China's experts, because Marxist economic philosophy was of no help in diagnosis.

The search for causes proceeded in two stages. The first (1976-1979) was dominated by political housecleaning and ideological score settling. All the economy's disabilities were blamed on the erroneous, ultraleftist machinations of the Gang of Four—as Mao's wife Jiang Qing and her three allies derisively came to be known. Later, Mao's own policy mistakes after 1957 also were targeted for blame. This approach implied that there was nothing wrong with the PRC's basic economic system that a change in personnel and in "style of work" could not fix. China's economic ills were thought to be due to incorrect policies, deviations from proper socialist conduct, and the cannibalization of economic institutions by recurrent mass campaigns. China's economic problems, in other words, were to be found not in the socialist model of command (central) planning but in the defective use of the model.

One difficulty with this diagnosis was that other communist economies were suffering identical ills, although none of them had endured the policy errors of Mao and the Gang of Four. All of them, however, had their origins in the same Stalinist plan. This prompted the more perceptive Chinese economists in 1979 and 1980 to conclude that the chief cause of China's economic ills was not the defective application of the socialist model, but the structure of the centrally planned economy borrowed from the Soviets.

Such discovery was fraught with peril because it implicitly but unavoidably questioned the very foundations and essence of the socialist economic system. In Marxist-Leninist terms, the discovery was more than merely revisionist; it bordered on the counter-revolutionary.

Despite the negative implications for socialism, the idea that the main source of China's economic troubles lay in its adoption of the Soviet economic system began to take hold in 1979. Permeating theoretical discussion, the idea increasingly found expression in muted calls for reform of the system itself, rather than mere adjustment of policies.

Remedies: Two Choices

PRC leaders recognized that, conceptually, there were two kinds of remedies to correct the economic ills that had been identified in the post-Mao years.

The first remedy consisted of intrasystemic changes. These were, in essence, policy changes or "adjustments" that could be far-reaching but did not alter the institutional structure of the centrally planned economy. Operationally, possible such adjustments were: a) administrative reorganization and reshuffling of goal priorities, and b) borrowing various techniques from market systems and using them as supplements to the central plan. Using capitalist techniques to build socialism is of course based on the assumption that the use of markets and private property is separable from the pluralistic economic culture and ethical system within which they were conceived.

COCO
China Times
Taipei

Reprinted with permission.

The second type of remedy consisted of reforms that address the institutional structure and principles of the basic economic system. Such reforms change the plan to the point where market relations and *de facto* private property rights become the system's dominant organizational arrangements—in other words, they involve the marketization and privatization of command. Allocative decision-making power is vested in consumers and producers directly linked by competitive market transactions. The transactions are voluntary, based on the maximization of profits by producers and of satisfactions by consumers, both calculated by reference to flexible market prices. Reform, then, is intersystemic change—in Marxist terms, "capitalist restoration." The plan is decentralized in an economic sense....

Marketization and privatization have an internal logic that makes it essential for the process to continue and expand once it is set in motion. The history of the agricultural contract system illustrates this. The one to three year lease of land to households gave rise to underinvestment and an abusive use of land. After all, there is little incentive for a family to invest in a landholding that in a year or so will pass to someone else. This disincentive forced Beijing to extend the term of the leases under *baogan daohu* [farming contracts] to fifteen to twenty years.

It was the same story with draft animals. Rotating them among households resulted in animals that were overworked and underfed. The response was to permit peasant families to own livestock. Today 90 percent of draft animals in China are owned privately by peasant households. Because there were similar difficulties with the collective tractors, their ownership was made private. Peasants also eventually were allowed to purchase trucks or to use their tractors for transportation. In time, some households began to specialize in transportation and machinery repair. Many such specialized households have come into being in farm-related activities (poultry raising, grain production, fish breeding), services (farm machinery operations), and manufacturing and processing of goods (furniture, clothing, construction materials, food processing).

Successful Agricultural Reform

These specialized occupations and township-run mini-industries have provided employment for the large numbers of workers who no longer are needed to till the land because of the responsibility system's increased farm productivity. Collective workshops, meanwhile, have been rented to family cooperatives or individuals, who run them more efficiently than did the township bureaucrats.

To achieve economies of scale, land parcels assigned to individual households can now be consolidated. Compensation is made for investments improving the productivity of the land. Some family tenant farms are now as large as 150 acres, and a family with such a farm is allowed to hire a limited number of workers to help with farm operations.

Investment in land and in private business requires credit. As such, credit and marketing cooperatives now thrive.

There is no doubt that the pace of marketization and privatization in the countryside has accelerated since the early 1980s and that its scope has expanded. While conditions vary from place to place, it is clear that in this sector of the economy adjustment is near to, if it has not already crossed, systemic borders.

Wide-Open Opportunity

There is a sense of wide-open opportunity, not only in the countryside, where the state is decollectivizing agriculture, but also in the cities, where private shopkeepers eagerly sell goods that are more stylish and colorful than those in state stores. Most surprising of all, there is a tangible sense of entrepreneurship and increasing wealth. With virtually no capital, formerly unemployed laborers begin by selling on street corners and end up opening their own shops. Peasants are forming their own trucking companies. The bold are quickly being rewarded. In a short period, it is possible to become a relatively rich merchant.

Merle Goldman and Marshall I. Goldman, *The New York Times*, July 24, 1984.

To a significant extent, China's agriculture has been freed from the fetters of a centrally planned economy. The results have been spectacular in terms of production, productivity, and per capita income. Since 1978, rural per capita income has risen almost 250 percent. Grain output has increased from 280 million tons in 1977 to 400 million tons in 1983. Roughly one-third of rural labor has been released for other tasks and absorbed into mostly private or private-cooperative service and manufacturing operations. Moreover, the average rural diet has improved.

Premier Zhao Ziyang announced this year that the state gradually would cease being the only purchaser of key agricultural products. Disappearing with this will be the last vestiges of state quotas and pricing in the agricultural sector. This, again, is a logical outcome of the marketizing and privatizing process initiated in 1979. As a result of this process, output increased to the point where quotas are not needed; more is being offered than the state can handle, and in some instances, the state-set quota price is higher than the market-determined price for the same products. Under the new system, family farmers are no longer guaranteed a basic income from quota sales to the state, but they gain greater latitude in decision-making. They can branch out into production lines dictated by their own perception of the market situation. They take the risks, and they reap the benefits....

Reforming PRC industry and commerce will be difficult. The changes involved affect the highly bureaucratized state sector of the economy at the central and provincial levels. Opposition to granting firms expanded decision-making responsibilities will come not only from the supervisory bureaucracies, but from the many managers who thrive within the existing system. They have little knowledge of, and less inclination for, competitive market behavior, economic risk taking and entrepreneurship....

What began as minor repair of the PRC's socialist economic system savaged by the radicalism of the Cultural Revolution has developed through the internal logic of the process into a serious attempt to restructure China's Soviet-type command economy. Marketization and privatization have advanced most in agriculture, albeit against determined opposition from sections of the party and bureaucracy. In this sector, systemic reform truly has begun.

Extending the rural changes to the urban industrial and commercial sector will prove far more difficult, because it involves the marketization of the present industrial wholesale and retail price system and a significant broadening of decision-making powers to local enterprises. Reform of urban industry and commerce requires a sharp reduction in the powers of the state and party economic bureaucracies. It calls for the mobility of labor and capital. Many bureaucratic managers are not willing or able to accept this level of privatization.

Half Measures

While the economic obtacles in the way of systemic reform are serious, the greatest danger comes from politics. Using capitalist techniques to build socialism is not a politically, ideologically, or ethically neutral question. Marketization and privatization of the institutional structure of the economy involve pluralization of decision-making, leading to the creation of competing power bases in society....

The experience of Hungary and Yugoslavia suggests that half measures do not resolve the kind of qualitative ills that centrally planned economies exhibit. In fact, a bit of market discipline and a dash of privatized property rights mixed in with a lot of bureaucratic planning and administrative controls make matters worse. There is no such thing as market socialism, if "socialism" means a centralized economic plan. Systemic reform cannot be limited to a single sector, but must apply to the entire, integrated institutional structure of the planned economy. While not inconceivable if the present leadership survives Deng's succession, the likelihood of such complete reform in China is small. Still, the PRC's central administrative command planning is so manifestly crippled that remedy would appear possible only by systemic reform in the direction of markets and private property.

U.S. interests are deeply involved with China's modernization.

At stake are significant commercial interests as well as strategic, political, and ideological considerations. It is in the U.S. interest that China's economy be market-oriented, that its domestic and international policies contribute to regional stability, and that its government and people eschew the excesses of Maoism.

"In Deng's China, Marxism-Leninism, or 'communism'...is alive and evolving. It may even be improving with age."

China Is Developing a New Form of Communism

William Sexton

William Sexton, the author of the following viewpoint, is a Western observer who believes that China is not turning its back on communism, but rather is developing a new form of communism. Mr. Sexton was chief of *Newsday's* Asia Bureau from 1979 to 1982, the years that China's reforms under Communist leader Deng Xiaoping began, and is currently an associate editor at *Newsday*. The recent reform is part of a long-term evolution in Chinese communism, Mr. Sexton argues, and should not be dismissed as simply another radical swing in China's internal politics.

As you read, consider the following questions:

1. Why is the West surprised by China's successes, according to the author?
2. What distinction does Mr. Sexton make between Deng's Marxist theories and Stalin and Mao's theories?
3. According to Mr. Sexton, Soviet-style central planning leads to shortages, poor merchandise, and low productivity. How do the Chinese plan to modify central planning?

William Sexton, "China Turns Loose a New Communism," *Newsday*, October 28, 1984.
© Copyright 1984, Newsday, Inc. Reprinted with permission.

Eighteen months ago [in 1983] my wife and I packed our bags, bade a relieved farewell to the *waijiao gongyu* (foreigners' apartment house) that had been our home in Peking, and headed home to the United States. We'd lived for nearly three years there in the diplomats' neighborhood known as *Jianguomenwai*, or Outside Build-the-Nation-Gate. *Jianguo* for short: Build-the-Nation.

No longer was there a gate, much less city walls. The Communists tore these down after their victory in 1949 (the walls had served their enemy, the Nationalists, all too well). During our years in Peking, Build-the-Nation became an expressway interchange and subway station, and broad Changanjie (Way of Eternal Peace) got a new overpass on its way to Tian An Men, the sprawling central square you're always seeing on television.

Our apartment was brand-new, too, a spacious and quite comfortable five rooms and two balconies on the seventh floor of a 15-story high-rise. (We'd been offered a more luxurious place on the 14th floor, but turned it down out of nervousness about Chinese elevators.) It was a great improvement over living in a hotel room, as we'd done for most of our first year.

Changes in Build-the-Nation

From the front of Building 7 (which, for some reason known only to the Chinese, was the back of the apartment), our view was a checkerboard of deep excavations and noisy construction sites. Dump trucks and mule-drawn wagons in an endless parade fed the concrete mixers and cranes that ran from 6 a.m. till 11 p.m.

From the living room, on the back of the building, we peered down through our picture windows into a sprawling outdoor workshop of plumbers, steamfitters and machinists, surrounded by uncovered stacks of radiators and toilet bowls and such. At least we always had hot water, and the elevator did work. And in the intervals between dust and storms and sieges of smog you could occasionally make out the lovely Fragrant Hills, China's Berkshires, on the western horizon.

We saw our former home again, pictured in a Chinese newsmagazine. Along with the big CSSX4 intercontinental missiles and the army's gaudy new uniforms, Build-the-Nation was being shown off in panoramic color on the occasion of China's 35th anniversary as a Communist state.

But the view came as a shock. So many other buildings had been finished, and parks and trees and flower beds emplaced, that we couldn't be sure which of the trim 15-story structures had been our home. In a year and a half they'd transformed the old neighborhood from a dusty construction site into a spacious garden community of luxury high-rises.

Why is it always such a surprise if China does something right? Chinese energy built Taiwan, Hong Kong, Singapore and the bustling Chinatowns of our own country. The same Confucian work ethic accounts in good part for the economic miracles of Japan and South Korea. China itself is the world's oldest living nation-state, a marvel of adaptation.

Yet inevitably we Westerners are surprised or suspicious—or both—if a Chinese missile flies, or Hong Kong wins a reasonable charter for its future, or, despite our qualms, the locally built elevators function without mishap. Why should this be?

That's easy. China is Communist, and Communists never get things right. This certainty is buttressed by ample remembrance of Chinese backwardness even before the Communists seized power: the Qing dynasty's terminal chaos, the bestiality of the successor warlords, recurring drought and destruction during the civil war and, more recently, the manic campaigns of Chairman Mao Tse-tung. Small wonder the 19th century's "sick man of Asia" image comes so much more readily to mind than Napoleon's vision of a sleeping giant.

The giant stirred mightily [recently], judging from all the press it got.

Adapting to New Discoveries

We still believe in the socialist goal, in the goal of communism. China had [its] revolution through this theorem and Mao particularly has the credit of combining the Marxist theorem with China's realities....

The great scientists—be it Newton or be it Einstein—made great contributions in their field. But they did not say the truth just ends there. It has to be developed and adapted to the new discoveries and new developments, and so it is also in China's reality.

We have to develop how best to accelerate the production to improve the livelihood of the people. And right now we think it's for the people to judge whether that policy is right or wrong, and the standard is whether that policy helped people to have a better livelihood and better security.

Zhang Wenjin, *Los Angeles Times*, August 5, 1984.

The big story was that Deng Xiaoping's regime, having already abandoned doctrinaire collectivism in the countryside, was now resolved to do the same in the cities. The Central Committee of the Chinese Communist Party had so decreed.

No Sudden Lurch

Once again, the news was greeted with a good bit of surprise and doubt. After all, replacement of central planning with market forces is tantamount to demolishing a central pillar of Marxist-Leninist-Maoist thought. This must be another one of those Chinese zigs, to be followed sooner or later by yet another zag like Mao's cultural revolution. Would they never steady the compass and lock on course?

The truth is that...[the] momentous "decision" was no sudden lurch, but very much what Deng and his allies had in mind as far back as 1957. That's why they got into such trouble with Mao. The specific course had been decided by the Central Committee in 1978, as soon as Mao's chosen successors could be dealt with. All that happened...is that Deng went public.

True, Deng said, "We regard it as a kind of revolution." What Deng didn't say was that the revolution had already taken place, in a million party meetings and thousands of retirements and hundreds of promotions judiciously spaced over the half-dozen years since his own restoration to power—and in not a few prison terms, no doubt, for people who got too persistently in the way, like the Gang of Four.

Nothing made the fait accompli more evident than the pictures of Deng's heir-apparent, Party Secretary Hu Yaobang, at the parade celebrating the 35th anniversary of Mao's proclamation of the People's Republic. Perched atop the Gate of Heavenly Peace, where on Oct. 1, 1949, Mao declared, "China has stood up," Hu stood up himself—in a smartly tailored Western suit. Premier Zhao Ziyang was similarly clad. Only the older, passing generation— Deng, for one, and Chen Yun, the elderly Shanghai economist who'd been planning this from the very beginning—wore Mao suits. It was no coincidence.

Marxist Evolution

That is Deng's way, manipulating the symbols so vital to Chinese consciousness; plotting, just like a chess grandmaster, a hundred moves ahead of the next; appearing to waver if there is opposition, pausing to rally public opinion to his cause and only then pressing ahead; enshrining his victories with great public occasions—and thus, in his twilight years, reshaping an entire nation's ideas to his and Chen Yun's design.

The new news...perhaps, was this: that in Deng's China, Marxism-Leninism, or "communism" in the shorthand of the West, is alive and evolving. It may even be improving with age. Think of the quandary it poses to the 400-odd Russians holed up in the big Soviet Embassy compound.

There are more than 1 billion Chinese, nearly four times the number of Soviet citizens; the two giants share a 4,000-mile frontier, and China's economy grows while the Soviet Union's stagnates. The two nations are not, to be sure, in the same league militarily or economically, but ideologically the torch of Marxist evolution—that's evolution, not revolution—seems to have passed out of Moscow's hands. Moscow's chief reaction is to deploy 50 Soviet divisions along the Chinese frontier, roughly equal to the force facing NATO troops.

What does Deng know that eludes Konstantin Chernenko? What Deng knows is that a state is no stronger than its economy (good Marxism, that), that only hard work builds the economy, and that you have to make it fun for people to work hard. Marx thought they'd do it on principle, Lenin thought they could be organized into it, Stalin tried force and Mao employed slogans. Deng is using money, and things to spend that money on. It's not quite correct to call this capitalism, since the state retains title to all land and most enterprises. But neither, certainly, is it what most of us call communism.

A Third Road

Rather, Deng's men are fashioning a third road, picking and choosing from history's offerings much as America's founding fathers did. It's hardly the political mix that Westerners would select, but neither are China's requirements very Western.

Ravaged by a century of foreign invasion, civil war and internal decay, China set out in 1949 to rebuild itself on the Lenin-Stalin economic model, in which the state plan decrees what each factory will build, what each store will sell and what each person will earn. Quotas and subsidies provide the motive force.

China's Goal

There is, of course, the ideological desire to prevent the growth of a Capitalist "class" in the People's Republic of China, which, after all, remains a Marxist state. In contrast to appearances created by China's continuing pragmatic moves toward individual financial incentives and a "freer" marketplace, the long-term goal is still Communism, not Capitalism.

John A. Reeder, *Columbia Journal of World Business*, Fall 1984.

For a backward country lacking the skills and savings that capitalism requires, the model looked good in theory. But Soviet experience proves after seven decades that following it produces not the predicted utopia but a realm of shortage, shoddy merchandise, low productivity and ubiquitous corruption.

China proposes to keep central planning for strategic materials like steel and fossil fuels, but to abolish the quotas and subsidies that distort commerce elsewhere. Instead, real prices will govern distribution. ("We Marxists do not envy you capitalists your recessions and unemployment," a Hungarian central planner said a few years ago, "but your price mechanism is mighty useful.")

The problem for Marxists is how to let go of the tiger's tail that subsidies and quotas have become, a problem with which American farmers have some familiarity. If, say, the commodity is rice, how do you eliminate the subsidy and let the price reach its natural level without endangering social order? The answer is: Very carefully.

Cautious Innovations

In a draft program that had been circulated for years before its [recent] public adoption..., the Central Committee was indeed careful. "As the reform of the price system affects every houeshold and the national economy as a whole, we must be extremely prudent, formulate a well-conceived program based on the growth of production and the capability of state finances and on the premise that the people's real income will gradually be increased, and then carry it out in a planned and systematic way," the formal document states. "...This reform is an exploratory and innovative undertaking by the masses and it is very complex. We must not try to accomplish the whole task at one stroke."

That's what the Central Committee says, but you can bet all the steps already have been planned to the closest details, the key actors already put into position, the legislation and regulations and instruction manuals ready to roll on a thousand printing presses. Successful innovators will be vaulted from nowhere into top jobs, as Zhao Ziyang was from governor of Sichuan to prime minister of China.

That's how Deng went about transforming China's agriculture in the space of five years, dismantling Mao's huge communes and restoring the individual family to its central role in farming. It was all in the plan, and the plan worked.

As we learned in Build-the-Nation, life within a transforming society can be noisy and messy. If the machinery is overloaded it can be downright perilous. That makes it unlikely given the tremendous effort just to hold a country of 1 billion together, that today's Chinese will enjoy the Western luxuries we call human rights. There may even be more repression than less during the nervous time of dismantling one economic structure and erecting another.

Most Chinese, probably, will happily settle for a better material life—for now. Dealing with the tiger's tail of repression can wait.

Modernization Instead of Revolution

The immediate challenge, therefore, isn't to throttle dissent, although the plainclothes thugs of the Bureau of Public Peace stand ready and willing. It's to keep living standards edging steadily upward so there'll be no cause for opposition.

"For the first time since 1949," Hunter College's Donald S. Zagoria, an expert on Soviet and Chinese politics, recently wrote in *Foreign Affairs*, "the revolutionaries are being replaced by modernizers. And to modernize China now requires a long period of external peace and internal stability." And, it might be added, a readjustment of world trade to make room for its exports.

In the immediate future, Taiwan is probably less of a danger to Sino-American relations than the new barriers to Chinese textiles. As for the very long range, surely all geopolitical bets are off if Deng succeeds. "If," indeed....

"The Mandate of Heaven"

In the symbolic vocabulary of China's long history, good times represent "the mandate of heaven," and a dynasty that loses this mandate loses the right to rule. Keeping the good times going is by no means assured for Deng and his successors.

"The Congolese...increasingly recognize that a period of lucrative capitalism will be necessary to fund their egalitarianism."

The Failure of Communism in Africa's Congo

Justine De Lacy

After gaining independence from the West, some African countries adopted Marxist economic systems in an effort to get rid of the remaining effects of colonialism and equitably develop their countries. Africa's persistent poverty has led some Marxist nations to adopt capitalist measures. In the following viewpoint, Justine De Lacy details the failure of communism in a small West African country, the Congo. Ms. De Lacy is a free-lance writer living in Paris. This viewpoint is taken from an article she wrote for *The Atlantic Monthly*.

As you read, consider the following questions:

1. Why did agricultural production drop after the tripartite committees started running them, according to Ms. De Lacy?
2. Why does the author consider the Congo's reliance on revenue from oil exports dangerous?
3. How does Marxism benefit the Congolese, according to the author?

Justine De Lacy, "Western Investors Now Welcome," *The Atlantic Monthly*, January 1984.

Mention the Congo, and most people think of the former Belgian Congo, Conrad's Heart of Darkness, the vast, mineral-rich land that is present-day Zaire. Yet just across the Congo River lies "another" Congo, the small but strategically located People's Republic of the Congo, a former French colony, where one of black Africa's more interesting political and economic evolutions is under way.

In 1963, three years after winning its independence from France, this Central African country of 1.6 million, which lies between Gabon and Zaire and borders on the oil-rich Angolan province of Cabinda, became the first African country to proclaim a "Marxist orientation" and sign a military-cooperation treaty with the Soviet Union. Two years later, the United States and Great Britain closed their embassies. As foreign-owned companies were nationalized, Western investors left, and Cuba began using the Congo as a conduit for arms to Angola. So many Chinese arrived, ostensibly to complete construction projects, that alarmed neighbors accused the Congo of helping foreign powers to "destabilize Africa."

Marxist Failure

After twenty years of "scientific socialism," the People's Republic of the Congo is making public the extent to which many of its socialist experiments have failed. Behind an elaborate facade of Marxist rhetoric, President Denis Sassou-Nguesso, forty, a handsome, French-educated man whose three-piece suits are so well cut that the French press calls him the "Marxist dressed by Cardin," is carrying out a carefully orchestrated rapprochement with the West. The country that was once hard-line enough to be called the "Albania of Africa" appears to be switching allegiance from Marx to Adam Smith.

In Brazzaville, the capital, a sleepy city with sand-gouged streets, portraits of Marx and Lenin vie for space with Mercedes ads, and grocery stores are stocked with foie gras and champagne. Streets are lined with late-model Toyotas, and the nouvelle cuisine at the Arc-en-Ciel would surely rate two stars from Michelin if the restaurant were in Paris. A few Congolese even wear shirts printed with dollar signs.

The about-face began in 1979, when Sassou-Nguesso, a colonel in the Congolese Army, came to power. Sassou-Nguesso reversed the trend that had begun in 1963, when the Congo's first socialist president, Alphonse Massamba-Debat, jettisoned the democratic government that had been in place since independence, adopted a policy of "scientific socialism," and established a single-party state. The regime did not, however, become militantly Marxist until the 1968 coup d'état led by Marien Ngouabi, a popular captain in the parachutist corps, who ruled from 1968 until his mysterious murder, in 1977....

Cumbersome state farms and newly nationalized state companies, directed by tripartite committees of workers, managers, and party members (the *"trilogie déterminante"*), were set up according to the standard Eastern-bloc model. Soon mismanagement, lack of discipline, and overstaffing had disastrous effects on production. Sugar output at the Suco sugar plantation, nationalized in 1970, fell from a record 100,000 tons in 1968 to 5,700 tons a decade later. In 1977, the Suco refinery shut down, forcing the Congo, once a large-scale sugar exporter, to import sugar for domestic needs. Under the

---

Living Like Capitalists

The Congo allows considerable free commerce. "Here there is no trouble," says Jimmy, who has been in the paint business in Africa for thirty-eight years. "The government encourages investment. Here I am a socialist and a communist and a capitalist. The people are'—and up goes his thumb. He is so happy in the Congo, he says, that he recently bought a bar and restaurant in the capital city of Brazzaville, and has encouraged his son, just finishing school in Europe, to settle in Brazzaville and run it....

As Nicole Brenier, economic officer at the U.S. embassy, puts it, "They are Marxists, but not living like Marxists. Nothing is Marxist in the culture here. They are living like capitalists." Adds John Archibald, another U.S. diplomat in the Congo, "It's like day and night with Zaire. The economy here is working. The people are happy. The policy is very pragmatic. They're not dumb. Who needs enemies?"

Jonathan Kwitny, *Endless Enemies: The Making of an Unfriendly World*, 1984.

French, who had ruled the Congo since the 1880s, the Niari Valley had regularly produced large harvests of such lucrative export crops as coffee, cocoa, palm oil, peanuts, and tobacco. But artificially low government-controlled prices, a characteristic of Eastern-bloc economics, soon discouraged the private farmers, who account for 70 percent of the Congo's agricultural production. As groves went uncared for, citrus and banana production fell. Peanut-oil plants had to close because the few peasants who continued to grow peanuts sold them on the black market for twice the government-controlled price. Also in decline were exports of tropical hardwoods from the equatorial forest that covers two thirds of the Congo.

Without maintenance, the Congo-Océan Railway—the sole link between Brazzaville and Pointe-Noire, which is the country's only port, some 250 miles away—began to fall apart. By 1979, state companies had accumulated a debt of 88 billion CFA francs, or $225 million. (The Congo, along with Chad, Cameroon, Gabon, and the Central African Republic, is a member of a five-nation franc zone whose common currency, the CFA franc, is backed by the French treasury and pinned to the French franc at a rate of fifty to one.) State farms were such a failure that food imports were costing the

Congo $48 million a year. The country still had only 300 miles of paved roads. Oil revenues, from deposits discovered in 1957, helped delay collapse by offsetting the deficits. However, when disputes with foreign operating companies over taxes led to a drop in production (the 1975-1977 output was projected at 14 million tons, but only 6 million were produced), the government was forced to scale down ambitious development plans. Ngouabi blamed the oil companies and vowed to "get the foreign opportunists who had sabotaged the Congo's future."

Wooing Western Investors

Shortly after this proclamation, he was assassinated, under circumstances that are still unclear (five days later, the Archbishop of Brazzaville, the last person to have seen Ngouabi alive, was also killed). In 1979, the Central Committee deposed Ngouabi's successor, General Yhombi-Opango, and imprisoned him for corruption...; it elected Sassou-Nguesso, the vice president, to succeed him....

Surprisingly, Sassou-Nguesso immediately set about wooing the Western investors who had been alienated by Ngouabi's policies. In a dramatic reversal of the 1972 Second Party Congress, which had listed "elimination of the private foreign sector" as one of its aims, Sassou-Nguesso assured private investors that no further nationalizations or Draconian taxes on private enterprise were planned. Moreover, he has soothed qualms about the Congo's continuing ties with the Soviet Union and Cuba by stating that the Congo has no wish to "export its ideology" or to serve as a "base for the destabilization of Africa." Shortly after he came to power, Sassou-Nguesso expressed a desire for "increased cooperation with the petroleum industry." As a result of his overtures to French and Italian operating companies, the Congo today is black Africa's fourth largest oil producer, after Nigeria, Gabon, and Angola.

The increase in oil production improved the Congo's economic position considerably; from 1978 to 1982, the country increased its trade surplus from $16 million to $250 million, and oil currently accounts for 88 percent of the country's foreign-exchange earnings. Production in 1982 was 4.3 million tons, one and a half times the 1979 total, and was largely responsible for the Congo's $1,200 per capita annual income, high by African standards. Soon after Sassou-Nguesso took over power, accreditation was granted to the first American ambassador to the Congo in fourteen years.

The edging away from the East is most pronounced in the economic sphere. Inefficient state companies—whose debts are still the biggest drag on the economy—are being broken up and told to pay their way, and nine will soon be closed. In a major departure from the socialist practice of putting full employment ahead of profits, the government recently laid off 760 workers at the Suco sugar plantation. This year, the tripartite management committees in twelve state companies will be replaced by capitalist-style corporation heads who will have the power to hire and fire....

The Congo has stopped trying to bail out the state farms set up by Ngouabi—"They are a disaster," Marius Mouambenga, the minister of agriculture, says. Most seed and machinery and the largest share of available credit are now being directed to the private sector. Food prices are slowly being raised in an effort to stimulate production....

French Influence

Encouraged by the current climate of political stability and economic reform, Western investors are responding to Sassou-Nguesso's overtures. The first to take advantage of the new investment opportunities have been the French, the Congo's old colonial masters. The number of French people working in the Congo has doubled in the past two years—at present, the total is about 8,000—and France now holds a controlling interest in about 30 percent of the economy and provides 65 percent of the imports. Starting at Ouesso, a bush town nine days upriver from Brazzaville, where little girls sell peanut butter wrapped in banana leaves, the French firm Ducler is putting one of the world's most expensive roads through the dense equatorial forest. The 600-kilometer road, which is expected to cost $1 million per kilometer and which will take six years to complete, will allow tropical hardwoods to be transported to the coast in twenty-four hours—rather than the months required to float logs down the river....

Relations between the two countries are good, generally, and the Congo has little of the colonial "complex" that plagues the relations of many African states with their former rulers. The capital is still named after its French founder, Savorgnan de Brazza; French is still

Bas, Greece

the official language; and little effort has been made to Africanize official dress. The Congolese, however, are anxious to diversify contacts, especially in offshore oil exploration. "The number of contacts we have with France is not a question of preference but of volume based on history," Emmanuel Yoka explains. "I speak French, I wear suits, I eat cheese. All that will remain. It's our minds we must keep free."

The diversification seems to be under way. Italy controls AGIP, the Congo's other foreign-operated oil company, and two American oil companies, Cities Service and Coastal, are currently involved in further oil exploration. U.S. imports from the Congo have more than doubled in the past two years and now are valued at some $600 million; the United States is the largest buyer of Congolese oil, taking 80 percent of what is produced. In turn, the Congo has "significantly increased its American imports," according to a U.S. Embassy official....

Lack of Soviet Aid

This cordiality toward the West is largely the result of Sassou-Nguesso's disgruntlement about the lack of Soviet aid. The Comecon countries buy less than 6 percent of the Congo's exports and provide a mere 3.5 percent of their imports. ("We'd *like* to buy Russian tape recorders," the manager of the central bank says with a grin. "But there just don't seem to be any.") Though the Soviet Union is the Congo's main military supplier—twelve Soviet MIG 21s are visible as you fly over Pointe-Noire—its aid has consisted mostly of selling at inflated prices outdated military equipment and machinery for which the Congolese can get no spare parts. The Soviets built a 100-bed maternity hospital in 1966, and completed the 120-bed Cosmos Hotel in 1969. The latter was so poorly run that it closed in January of 1983, for lack of business. Its management is being taken over by Frantel, the French hotel chain. "For twenty years, the Congo has been ideologically committed to the Soviet Union and has gotten nothing in return," says a French diplomat. Despite the various cooperation treaties, relations between the Russians and the Congolese have never been chummy. The Soviets are regarded as racists who stick to themselves and never have any money. ("Don't ride a bicycle," I was advised during a recent visit, "or people will think you are Russian and no one will talk to you.") This coolness has intensified since Sassou-Nguesso's trip to the Soviet Union in 1981, during which the Russians made it clear that they had no intention of participating in his development plans. ("The Soviet Union's African policy is not hard to figure out," says a French official. "They take care of the ideology and leave the economy up to the West.") The Soviets have also angered the Congolese recently by poaching on fishing beds off Pointe-Noire and by shipping minerals to the USSR for "evaluation" and then offering a "take-it-or-leave-it" price. Samples from a gold mine sent to the Soviet Union for analysis have never been returned, and some Congolese accuse the Russians of having stolen them. Though 400 Soviet teachers and advisers are still in the Congo, and large delegations from the Soviet Union, East Germany, and Czechoslovakia that arrive every other week at Brazzaville's Maya Maya airport are wined and dined in style, the atmosphere is far

---

Free Enterprise

Among Third World states there are a few who've found the secret of rapid growth and high living standards. The key is capitalism.

Although it gets little play in major press, there are free market countries in the Third World. A few adopted pro-market strategies at independence. Others turned to free enterprise when their Socialist economies collapsed. Together, these nations have posted astonishing economic gains; gains that prove that the market can produce prosperity as surely for Asians, Latins and Africans as it does for Americans.

Dan Dickinson, *Human Events*, January 21, 1984.

---

different from what it was in the days when the Soviets blithely used the Congo to infiltrate Angola. The Congo recently refused a Russian request for permission to build a deepwater port off Pointe-Noire, and the Cubans who used to train the President's bodyguards have been replaced by French instructors....

The Plan

One feature of socialist economic theory that the Congo has not abandoned is belief in a planned economy. "The Plan is the affair of all the people," reads one of the red billboards near the airport. Under the current $2.5 billion 1982-1986 Plan, oil money is being used to develop other sectors of the economy, such as fishing and forestry, in preparation for the day when the oil runs out. One third of the current investment credits are going to the construction of roads, jetties, and bridges on the Congo's many rivers, in an effort to open the way to the underdeveloped north (the *"désenclavement"* one hears about so much...) and thereby link the economy to the Congo's nearly inexhaustible wood supply. Up to [now]..., timber has accounted for only 5 percent of the earnings from exports, because the largest forests have been inaccessible.

The new roads will also provide a way for peasants to get their goods to market. Until the Ouesso road is completed, the only way to get goods out is by barge (and that route is closed when the Sangha River is dry, which normally means during five months of the year) or by plane (and airplanes cannot land on the red-clay airstrip when it rains). By boosting rural incomes in the expectation that they will eventually match urban incomes, the government is hoping to stop the flow of people to the cities and encourage farming. Many of the country's other plans for the future depend on the success of this policy, since the Congo already has one of Africa's most highly urbanized populations. Two thirds of the population live on 7 percent of the land, and only .6 percent of the territory is under cultivation. The Congo also has one of Africa's best-educated populations: 89 percent of all children attend school until the age of fourteen....

Foreign Trade Problems

The Congo still imports nearly half of its food. (One of the biggest imports is wheat, used to make the skinny baguettes of French bread one sees everywhere. Though the 50,000 tons of wheat the Congo imports annually are using up a sizable chunk of its foreign reserves, the government fears that the Congolese would riot if they couldn't get white bread, which is gradually supplanting cassava as the main starch food. They have also acquired from the French a taste for refined sugar. Huge sacks of brown sugar sit at the Suco plant, unexportable because of a world sugar glut and unsalable at home because the Congolese prefer white sugar, imported from France.)

Sixty-five percent of the Plan is financed by oil revenues, with the rest coming from foreign investment and aid. Since 1982, when oil prices began to fall (from $34 a barrel to the current price of $28.75), catching small Third World producers like the Congo off guard, the dangers of having an economy based on a natural resource whose world price fluctuates have become evident. Oil revenues are down 40 percent, and in November, Sassou-Nguesso appeared on television to announce cutbacks in the Plan beyond those announced earlier in the year.

Widespread ill health, due to poor nutrition, and a high infant-mortality rate prevail, and one frequently sees families chanting mourning rites on their way home from the ''Clinic of Death,'' as the Brazzaville hospital is known. Yet health care has received only $64.5 million under the current Plan (about 3 percent of all the projected Plan expenditures)....

Marxism's Future

Nonetheless, the extent of economic cooperation with the West has sparked talk of neocolonialism. Is the Congo edging away from the Eastern bloc only to ally itself with the former colonial powers on which many African nations have been blaming their troubles for years? And how can its Marxist ideology be reconciled with the current enthusiasm for marketing and profits? The answer to both questions boils down to pragmatism, by which the Congolese mean putting economics ahead of politics. While they are ideologically committed to socialism—''a society where man is not exploited by man'' is the way they usually explain it—they increasingly recognize that a period of lucrative capitalism will be necessary to fund their egalitarianism. To put the matter more simply, they've got to make money before they can begin redistributing it....

Marxism provides language and rituals capable of uniting a country that might otherwise dissolve into self-destructive factions. "It gives the Congolese a sense of belonging to something bigger than their region or their tribe, a sense they could not get from a more pluralistic society," explains a French diplomat. "Its strength is the one-party system. With more democracy, every tribe would demand its own party."

Private Investment

The people of the Congo are clearly benefiting from open competition, and from the encouragement of private investment with guarantees of no government interference. Congolese president Denis Sassou-N'Guesso has issued a standing call for private investment in such practical activities as agricultural exportation, animal raising, forestry, mining, small industry, hotel and restaurant construction, and tourism.

Jonathan Kwitny, *Endless Enemies: The Making of an Unfriendly World*, 1984.

But others feel that the veneer of Marxism will eventually disappear. "It must, because they are setting up a system to feed people and they know now that Marxism cannot do that," says another French diplomat, expressing a sentiment recently echoed by the minister of agriculture. "We must go with what works," says Marius Mouambenga. "If Marxism feeds the people, fine. But Marxism without revenue is Marxism without a future."

"African underdevelopment is...a result of the capitalist development of the West."

Capitalism Has Damaged Africa's Economy

Amechi Okolo

The West's impact on the economies of small African nations can be immense, a point developed in the following viewpoint by Amechi Okolo, a lecturer in International Relations at the University of Ife in Nigeria. He argues that beginning with the industrial revolution, Western capitalism has exploited Africa's natural resources through trade and kept the continent in poverty while the West has grown richer. Mr. Okolo has a doctoral degree from Purdue University.

As you read, consider the following questions:

1. On what basis does Mr. Okolo conclude that African poverty is caused by human forces?
2. What does the author mean by "unequal exchange" and how have unequal exchanges hurt Africa and helped the West?
3. What is the difference between undevelopment and underdevelopment, according to Mr. Okolo?

Africa and the International Political System, Timothy M. Shaw and Sola Ojo (eds), excerpts from "The Role of International Trade in the African Political Economy," Amechi Okolo, pp. 68-95. Copyright 1982 by University Press of America, Inc. Reprinted with permission.

In essence, both the development of the West and the under-development of Africa constitute the two sides of the development and dynamics of capitalism. As the umbilical cord linking the two economies, international trade facilitates one (the West) to develop while the other (Africa) stagnates and underdevelops.

The most striking feature of the contemporary African political economy is its abject poverty. The continent is notoriously poor with its members numbered amongst the lowest ranks inter-nationally along the conventional indices of "development." In Africa many people are literally dying of starvation and wretched-ness, many cannot afford cloth for their bodies, disease is rampant and death rates are the highest in the world....

Underdeveloping Slum

Moreover, despite the present level of wretchedness, the dimen-sions of human misery are multiplying in Africa geometrically. Africa is a disorganized society. She is not the "developing" con-tinent that most popular literature would want us to believe, but rather an "underdeveloped and underdeveloping" slum where the harsh realities of human existence are most evident. All the coun-tries of Africa have been categorised into the Third World group (with the significant exception of South Africa) based on their level of development. But recently it has become necessary and fashionable to subdivide them into Fourth and possibly Fifth Worlds based on their degrees of wretchedness and proximity to extinction.

Yet Africa is by no means a poor continent; in fact she is one of the richest continents on earth. Her soil is extremely rich but the products from below and above her surface have enriched other parts of the globe rather than her own peoples. Africa has an im-pressive range of resources of most of the world's major minerals. Her iron ore reserves are about twice those of the United States and two-thirds those of the Soviet Union based on an estimated two billion metric tons. Her petroleum reserves are perhaps unequalled anywhere and she pumps virtually all of them to the West. Take the Nigerian case as an example. Of the 2.5 billion barrels of Nigerian oil produced in 1976, 2.1 billion barrels were shipped to the West; and she exports the second largest amount of foreign oil to the U.S. next to Saudi Arabia.

In some instances Africa is the only known source of certain vital strategic minerals like chrome and uranium for the West. Her arable and pasture lands surpass those of the United States and the Soviet Union. She has over forty percent of the world's oceanic and hydroelectric power potential. And as solar energy emerges to become the next vital source of energy, Africa's share of global energy potential will become even greater. At present she supplies the West with oil to fuel its industrialised economy and in the future Africa—the tropical continent in the "colonial sun"—will be the main source of solar energy.

So Africa's poverty is not natural or inherent; instead, we are dealing with man-made poverty. She has all that it takes to be a great continent. She has the resources and the manpower of about 280 million people; yet most of her resources—human and material—have been devoted to the development of the West to her own detriment and underdevelopment. Linked to this increase in poverty as the striking feature of Africa's political economy is its extrovertedness.

Unequal Development

"Economic development" is a double-edged sword. As long as a capitalist world-economy exists, and we are part of it, the "economic development" of all zones simultaneously is inherently impossible, since the operation of the law of value requires that surplus be unequally distributed over the globe. The development of any one zone is therefore always at the expense of some other. World socialism cannot be defined by the phenomenon of less "developed" zones "catching up"....It involves rather the construction of a radically different mode of production, centering on production for use in an egalitarian, planned world, in which the states individually and the system of states collectively have both "withered away."

Immanuel Wallerstein, *Proletarianization and Class Struggle in Africa*, 1983.

An extroverted economy is one that exists primarily to service a foreign economy. All the important sectors of such an economy exist to service foreign interests. The African continent as a whole is organised to produce for export and whatever sparse rewards it receives from this production for export is again spent on foreign imports. Both the mechanisms of production for export and consumption of imports—that is, international trade—constitute a vital key to the understanding of African poverty. The logic of capitalism with its mechanisms of international trade has resulted in the "development of underdevelopment" in Africa, to use Andre Gunder Frank's phrase....

Inequality and exploitation have existed throughout human history. A few groups of people have always been able to acquire more than their share of a people's wealth and hence lord it over them politically and culturally. So society has always been divided into the "exploiters" and the "exploited" and the struggle between them has been the essential force of world history. In fact, as Marx sees it, "the history of all hitherto existing societies is the history of class struggles." So Marx sees exploitation and class struggles as not only inherent in history but as the very factors that *constitute* history. So we accept that man has always exploited man and that "whoever says organization says oligarchy."

188

The primary feature of exploitation through international trade is "Unequal Exchange" in the trade between the industrial nations and underdeveloped nations. Unequal exchange [occurs] when products involving the same amount of labor are rewarded unequally. The subsequent transfer of the surplus to another state causes one to stagnate while the other prospers. This means that products coming from Third World nations embody "hidden transfers" of surplus value to the West which causes the unequal development of the two groups.

So in trading with the West, Africa helped to develop Europe in the same proportion as Europe helped to underdevelop Africa. There is necessarily an inverse relationship between the development of one and the underdevelopment of the other. The uniqueness of labor power in contradistinction to other exchange commodities in a capitalist context exists because it is the only commodity which is capable of producing a value greater than its worth. In other words, labor power alone can produce its value plus something extra. This extra is the source of profit and this is what the capitalists keep in their companies and countries.

This uneven appropriation of the surplus value of labor power is the source of exploitation everywhere—in the industrial world as well as in the developing nations. However when dealing with international trade—that is, with cross-national trade—a new dimension is added. Within the boundaries of a state, the bourgeoisie appropriates this surplus value from the workers and hence exploits them. But this surplus remains within the nation so that, through a series of multiplier effects and leakages from the bourgeois class, some of the accumulated wealth eventually trickles down to the people, even if in unacceptable quantities.

Bourgeois Socialism

This trickle down happens in a number of ways. The government usually gets hold of a sizable amount and spends it on infrastructure—roads, public buildings, education, health care, etc.—and on the provision of other social services and amenities. The cases of highly-developed social services in Europe, and the government's involvement in very sophisticated inter-state highways in the United States are examples of this. Or some super-capitalists (usually called the millionaires or billionaires depending on their degree of success in exploiting the workers) will set up all sorts of charitable organizations and foundations to help the people. All these are attempts to redistribute national wealth. Though they may constitute reluctant concessions in response to worker agitation by the national bourgeoisie, nevertheless they help to increase general societal wealth. Such charitable and philanthropic activities help to improve the workers' welfare and thus moderate the perceptions of exploitation.

The important point for this analysis, though, is that most of these forms of bourgeois "socialism" would and could not have been possible if the accumulated wealth had not remained within the country even if it remained with the bourgeoisie at the "top" of the national ladder. Hence the importance of international trade in the study of development and underdevelopment is that it helps us to focus not on how each national bourgeoisie exploits the working class of another state—in short how one "nation" exploits another. Exploitation as a system of production and distribution goes on in every society; but in some societies the accumulated wealth stays within the society while in others it is transferred out, usually involuntarily. Where it remains within the boundaries of the state, attempts are made, however imperfect they might be, to redistribute it, thus improving the societal welfare by increasing national wealth and contributing to national development. In societies where the accumulated wealth is transferred outside the state, internal redistribution is impossible and exploitation becomes routine, leading to the full force of deprivation and underdevelopment....

Undeveloped vs. Underdeveloped

Historically the mere presence of national exploitation did not by itself bring about national underdevelopment. A nation could be "undeveloped" in contradistinction to being "underdeveloped." An undeveloped state occurs when the nation is unable to optimize the use of its human and natural resources. Therefore, it should be

Reprinted by permission: Tribune Media Services.

noted that the bulk of Africa was undeveloped before the march of capitalism on the continent. Also Europe was undeveloped before the industrial revolution. Before the Caucasian invasion of the North American continent, that area was also undeveloped.

From undevelopment, Western Europe and North America moved towards development, except for the few Indian reservations scattered across the United States. This means that the West was never underdeveloping. And comparing the Western state at that period to the situation of the African nations today overlooks the historical context of the Western nations at their undeveloped stage when there was no "developed" nation. The West was undeveloped at an historical epoch before the industrial revolution turned the wheels of progress. At the undeveloped stage the vast riches of the soil and sub-soil remained untapped and man was able to wring a subsistence existence directly out of nature....

Underdevelopment started when the industrial revolution released enormous potential for man to exploit and employ the resources of nature. For those societies which can exploit natural resources "better" than others, development is assured. Individual wealth is thereby increased and by arithmetical addition plus inter-action multiplier effects national wealth is also increased....

African underdevelopment is, then, a consequence of the world-wide expansion of capitalism and the integration of Africa into this international system.

International Trade

The cardinal role of international trade as the primary means by which African wealth is transferred to further develop the already "developed" West should be well understood. Without the international exchange of goods and services, the wealth generated by a society should accumulate and remain within it. Eventually some wealth might trickle down to the society so contributing to overall national development and social welfare....

In Africa the nations with a larger foreign trade sector relative to gross national product are the ones which suffer most and are most exploited through trade....

Third World nations with important rare resources benefit least from such advantages because:

(1) they become targets of major international rivalries;

(2) they are cornered into becoming mono-crop economies; that is, economies that depend on one product; and

(3) they typically get far less income for their products because a few multinational corporations usually control their production and marketing....

This [article] has tried to do three things. First, to sketch the development of capitalism stressing its inherent logic and dynamic which necessarily led to imperialism and colonialism. The logic of capitalism diminishes the rate of profit. To limit this, capitalists have expanded into Third World areas both for cheap labor and for raw materials. Second, to establish that African underdevelopment is as a result of capitalist development of the West. The development of the West and the underdevelopment of Africa constitute the two sides of a single phenomenon—what [Immanuel] Wallerstein calls the development of the "modern world-system."

Profits Before Hunger

As European countries colonized Africa, they disrupted African farming and herding systems that for centuries Africans had adapted to changing environmental conditions. Ecologically balanced food systems were undermined; the best agricultural lands were seized for growing coffee, sugar cane, cocoa and other export crops that would benefit Europe. Private and government investment went into developing these cash crops, while food production for the poor majority was neglected....

The forces that have institutionalized hunger in Africa are made up of African elites, multinational corporations, Western governments and international agencies....

The free market allocated food according to monetary wealth, not nutritional need. The six large corporations that control nearly 85 percent of world grain shipments are concerned with profits, not malnutrition. Thus we are confronted with the cruel irony that world grain reserves are at their highest levels in history, while famine stalks the African continent.

Kevin Danaher, *Utne Reader*, August/September 1985.

And third, finally, it is contended that international trade is the primary mechanism by which African wealth has been used to develop the West. Surplus value produced in Africa has been transferred to the West (now that outright brigandage and robbery are no longer used) in the form of "hidden transfers" and "unequal exchange."

"The Soviet Union stands for complete elimination of colonialism in all its forms and for national independence of all peoples."

Communism Supports Self-Determination

Vladimir Borisov

Communism as a doctrine views history as a progressive march which began in prehistory in communist societies and will eventually return to and culminate in a state of pure communism. For that reason, rebellions against communist governments are considered counterrevolutionary. Vladimir Borisov, a Soviet colonel and writer for *Soviet Military Review*, explains in the following viewpoint that Soviet aid to communist governments is not imperialism, but rather part of the USSR's international duty to further the cause of the communist revolutionary movement.

As you read, consider the following questions:

1. What is the Soviet "internationalist duty," according to Mr. Borisov?
2. What, according to the author, are the goals of the international proletarian struggle?
3. What is the imperialist reaction to the working people's struggles, according to the author?

Colonel Vladimir Borisov, "We Are Internationalists," *Soviet Military Review*, 1984, No. 11.

Fifty-three years ago, in 1931, a Soviet workers' delegation was on a trip through Europe. Among the delegates was Mariya Soboleva, one of the first women tractor drivers in the USSR. Here is what she later said about the trip. "As soon as we stepped on the pier the first thing the police would do was to isolate us from the workers. We were not allowed to visit plants, factories, workers' living quarters. However, when we came to Hamburg a German worker managed to sneak us to his home. When we entered the man took off a picture hanging on the wall and picked out a photograph of V. I. Lenin hidden in its back. The portrait was clipped from a newspaper. When we were about to leave he looked at us closely and asked: 'Will you hold out? You know, you are our last hope.' 'Don't worry, we shall stand firm' was our answer."

The Soviet people indeed held out, and they did much more. In the years after the revolution they built their country into a mighty industrial power, they turned it into a bulwark of progress and world security.

Western Imperialism

The road was not easy however. The imperialists of Germany, the United States, Britain, France, Japan and other states combined their efforts to strangle the young republic. They rushed economic, political and technical aid to the overthrown rulers of Russia, delivered arms to the counterrevolutionaries, and on top of that they sent massive regular army forces to intervene.

Building the foundation of the socialist society the Communist Party guided by V.I. Lenin raised a new army to defend the new state. The army was manned by people of all the nationalities living in Russia. In addition, over 250,000 internationalists— revolutionary-minded men and women from other countries, e.g. Poland, Hungary, Bulgaria, Germany, Mongolia, China, joined the ranks of the Red Army to defend the Soviet Republic.

Gratefully accepting a helping hand from the peoples of other countries, the Soviet Republic in turn did everything in its power to help the revolutionary movements of the working people in Finland, Germany, Austria and Hungary.

V. I. Lenin regarded the fraternal solidarity, mutual aid, joint defensive efforts of the working people of different nations a key to success in the struggle against world bourgeoisie, and he believed that the efforts to consolidate the power of the Soviets should be regarded as not just a national task, but as the internationalist duty of the working people and the best contribution to the world revolutionary movement.

Proletarian Solidarity

The internationalist nature of the Soviet Armed Forces manifested itself in the effective support it gave to the revolutionary liberation struggle in other countries. For instance, the Red Army rendered support to the people of Mongolia in 1921 to defeat the White Guard bands headed by General Ungern and to suppress the internal counterrevolutionary forces. In a sweeping operation at the Khalkhin-Gol River in 1939 combined Soviet and Mongolian forces routed a strong Japanese interventionist force.

The Soviet Union gave substantial political, moral, economic and military assistance to the working people of China in their struggle against the Japanese aggressors for national independence and freedom.

The USSR demonstrated its proletarian solidarity with republican Spain from 1936 to 1939. Over 3,000 Soviet volunteers fought in the ranks of the international brigades there.

The Soviet Union's adherence to its internationalist duty was unbending during the Great Patriotic War of 1941 to 1945. By breaking the back of the nazi aggressor the USSR not only preserved its freedom and independence, but it also accomplished a historic liberation mission. The defeat of nazi Germany and militarist Japan was a decisive contribution to the liberation of the conquered and oppressed nations of Europe and Asia.

Reared by the Leninist Communist Party, the Soviet Army emerged before the whole world as a true friend and protector of the working people, as an army of liberation, as a bearer of humanism and justice.

Social Progress

The Communists pay special attention to the anti-imperialist movements of the people, which have grown on an unprecedented scale and need a more solid organization and a clear understanding of the goals of their struggle, and to the building of socialism and communism, the main trend of social progress. Only Marxist-Leninist parties can give an answer to these and other burning questions of our time.

Nikolai Ovcharenko, *New Times*, May 1984.

Fighting side by side with the Soviet Army were Polish and Czechoslovak army units which had been formed on Soviet territory, as well as units of the People's Liberation Army of Yugoslavia, and later Bulgarian, Romanian and Hungarian army units. The total strength of the allied units raised in the USSR during the war exceeded 550,000.

The victory over nazi Germany demonstrated the superiority of the Soviet social system and proved the foresight and correctness of the CPSU's national policy, its allegiance to proletarian internationalism.

With the end of the Second World War socialism evolved beyond the frontiers of one country and became a world system.

Following the principles of proletarian internationalism, the USSR and other socialist states engaged in comprehensive economic, political and military cooperation. Pooling efforts in the tense international situation enabled them to negotiate many key economic and technological problems which facilitated the consolidation of the socialist system's defence capacity. In response to the aggressive North Atlantic bloc set up in 1949, the socialist states formed in 1955 the Warsaw Treaty Organisation. The Organisation embodied the primary Leninist ideas of proletarian internationalism, unity and cohesion of the fraternal nations in the defence of the revolutionary gains, in the defence of peace.

Even before the Warsaw Treaty was formally set up the Soviet Union had been rendering military support to socialist countries that were victims of imperialist aggression. In the 50s the US aggressive circles provoked war in Korea in an effort to do away with the Korean People's Democratic Republic. The KPDR gave a crushing rebuff to the aggressor which may largely be attributed to the prompt and massive Soviet aid in up-to-date materiel, arms and equipment.

The establishment of a defensive military-political alliance presented new and wider opportunities for a more effective and comprehensive collective security of the socialist community. Complying with its allied and internationalist duty and acting at the request of the government of Hungary, the Soviet Union extended a helping hand to the Hungarian working people in suppressing a counterrrevolutionary riot and preventing an imminent imperialist intervention.

Counterrevolutionary Encroachments

Responding to a request by the government of the GDR, the socialist states helped to rebuff in 1961 the West German revanchists who sought to change the status quo of Berlin, while a year later they forced the US imperialists to give up their plans to invade Cuba.

The vigorous support and the comprehensive assistance of the socialist states helped the people of Vietnam to emerge victorious from the protracted war of liberation and to rid the country of both the foreign invaders and their puppets.

Acting in concert, the socialist countries helped Czechoslovakia in August 1968 protect its socialist gains against counterrevolutionary encroachments.

The Soviet Union extends internationalist assistance to the Democratic Republic of Afghanistan. The people of Afghanistan are facing aggression, a kind of undeclared war, sponsored by the United States of America, Pakistan and some other states. In this critical situation the USSR responded to the call of the government of the DRA and, in compliance with the existing agreements and with the United Nations Charter, it has rendered the republic the necessary assistance.

The struggle of the peoples today is greatly facilitated by the very existence of a great socialist power, the USSR, which possesses tremendous political and economic potential. The Soviet Union stands for complete elimination of colonialism in all its forms and for national independence of all peoples.

Practical Deeds

The USSR is always on the side of the peoples fighting for socialism, peace, democracy and national sovereignty, and it proved this more than once by the practical deeds. For instance, the Anglo-French-Israeli aggression against Egypt was brought to a halt in 1956, and the imperialist invasion against Syria was timely prevented in 1957 mainly due to the firm and resolute posture of the USSR.

Disinterested Aid

The Soviet Union and other socialist states extend all-round and disinterested aid to the newly-free countries which chose the socialist way of development. If necessary, this aid extends to matters of national security and defence, as was the case with Angola and Ethiopia.

The imperialists are well aware of the power of international proletarian solidarity. That is why they stop at nothing to besmirch and discredit the very idea of proletarian internationalism. But their efforts are futile. *International solidarity of the working people is growing year by year and is becoming an ever more influential force in the*

world revolutionary movement.

The rapid growth of the forces of socialism and peace provokes rage and fury among the imperialists. The USA and its allies have openly set about preparing for a new world war. In this situation, the USSR, meeting the hopes and aspirations of the working people the world over, is doing everything in its power to fend off the threat of war, and preserve peace for the present and the future generations. And the Soviet Union is no longer alone in this fight, it is fighting hand in hand with all the socialist states, with all progressive forces throughout the world.

8 VIEWPOINT

"*The Red Empire...[has] a record of imperialist expansion unmatched by any 19th-century colonial power in its heyday.*"

Communism Destroys Self-Determination

Jack Wheeler

After World War II, some Third World revolutions were considered Marxist since they sought independence from the West and accepted Soviet aid. American conservatives believe Marxism's appeal is dying and point to the growing number of revolutions against Communist governments as evidence. In the following viewpoint, Jack Wheeler, director of the Freedom Research Foundation in La Jolla, California, argues that Soviet imperialism in the Third World is severely declining. Mr. Wheeler has a doctoral degree in philosophy.

As you read, consider the following questions:

1. How do Soviet economic problems contribute to Soviet imperialism, according to the author?
2. Why does the author believe that the guerilla wars being fought against the Soviets are of geopolitical significance?
3. What does Mr. Wheeler recommend US foreign policy be toward the Soviets?

Jack Wheeler, "Fighting the Soviet Imperialists: The New Liberation Movements," *Reason*, June/July 1985. Reprinted with the author's permission.

Today, the era of Western colonialism is over and only vestigial remnants of the great West European imperial empires remain, such as Gibraltar and French Polynesia. But while these empires vanished, one other—the last 19th-century colonial power left— had risen like a hideously deformed phoenix from revolutionary ashes and resumed its imperialist march once again.

World War II was supposedly fought, as was World War I in Woodrow Wilson's words, to make the world "safe for democracy." The result, however, was to make the world safe for Soviet imperialism. From 1939 to 1946, the Soviet Union expanded its official borders by over a quarter of a million square miles, 69,000 from Poland alone, and violently subjugated into colonies the whole of Eastern Europe.

Imperialist Expansion

Stalin's heirs have since tried to expand throughout what became known as the "Third World" by manipulating those movements and peoples trying to gain political independence from the West. On January 6, 1961, Soviet premier Nikita Khrushchev announced the Soviet government's formal support of "national liberation wars" in Africa, Asia, and Latin America as the means to achieve a communist (that is, Soviet) victory over the forces of capitalism (the United States). It was not until the 1970s, however, that this strategy really bore abundant fruit.

On the very last day of 1969, Brazzaville-Congo declared itself Africa's first Marxist-Leninist "People's Republic." Soviet-backed revolutionaries subsequently led Marxist-Leninist coups in South Yemen (1971), Benin (1972), Ethiopia (1977), the Seychelles (1977), Grenada (1979), and Surinam (1980). Cuban troops enabled the MPLA (Popular Movement for the Liberation of Angola) to seize power in Angola in 1975 and in 1979 did the same for the Sandinistas in Nicaragua. The coup in Portugal in 1974 allowed FRELIMO (Mozambique Liberation Front) to take over Mozambique without further struggle a year later. Also in 1975 the North Vietnamese army conquered South Vietnam in the name of the Viet Cong, and did the same for the communist group the Pathet Lao in Laos. (In the same year the China-backed Khmer Rouge took over Cambodia.) To close out the decade, the Soviet-armed Vietnamese army invaded Cambodia, chasing the genocidal Khmer Rouge into the jungles and installing a puppet regime, while the Red Army of the Soviet Union itself invaded Afghanistan. That's *14 countries* added to the Red Empire in little more than 10 years—a record of imperialist expansion unmatched by any 19th-century colonial power in its heyday.

That expansion, however, has come to an end. In this decade, the Soviets have not acquired a single new colony. Soviet influence throughout Africa has seriously eroded, sharply so in such client or quasi-client states as Guinea, Malagasay (Madagascar), and

Congo.

Why the halt in Soviet expansion? Because the Soviet Union, being not an economic superpower at all but merely the world's biggest banana republic, cannot back its empire up economically. Soviet Marxism, for every country that has embraced it, has become not a path to a glorious future but a one-way ticket to oppression and poverty. All the Soviets can offer, and what they have perfected, is what I call the Kremlin's "Franchise for Totalitarianism"—a modular formula applicable to any location whereby a small clique, even with no popular power base whatever, can gain and maintain a ruthless tyranny.

If you "buy" the franchise, the Kremlin will first supply you with massive amounts of military arms. For instance, when the Israelis invaded southern Lebanon in 1981 and captured Palestine Liberation Organization (PLO) arms caches stored there, they trucked out 4,700 truckloads of Soviet weaponry. Jonas Savimbi's anti-Marxist resistance movement in Angola, UNITA, is well-armed thanks substantially to South Africa's turning over to Savimbi the vast Soviet arms caches it captured in raids on encampments of the Soviet-sponsored South West Africa People's Organization (SWAPO) in southwest Angola.

Democratic Revolution

The Soviet Union and its proxies, like Cuba and Vietnam, have consistently supplied money, arms and training in efforts to destabilize or overthrow non-Communist governments. "Wars of national liberation" became the pretext for subverting any non-Communist country in the name of so-called socialist internationalism....

In recent years, Soviet activities and pretensions have run head-on into the democratic revolution. People are insisting on their right to independence, on their right to choose their government free of outside control. Where once the Soviets may have thought that all discontent was ripe for turning into Communist insurgencies, today we see a new and different kind of struggle: people around the world risking their lives against Communist despotism.

George Shultz, in a speech before the Commonwealth Club of California, February 22, 1985.

The instant you negotiate or seize a portion of governmental authority in the capital city, you request "fraternal assistance" to eliminate "counterrevolutionary elements." Within days, Soviet troop-transport planes will start bringing in Soviet-proxy troops, a service provided by the Cubans, for example, for the MPLA in Angola and the Sandinistas in Nicaragua.

Once any opposition to total government control is neutralized, then the franchise is set up in earnest. The Soviets supply ad-

201

ministrative personnel and "advisors" to each minister. The East Germans provide a palace guard and set up an internal spy and informer network of true Orwellian proportions. Terrorizing everyone from trusting any other fellow citizen—even brother and sister, parent and child—is the key to snuffing the development of any opposition and maintaining power.

Internal Repression

The Cubans supply the military manpower both to suppress any armed resistance and to prevent any rebellion from the military, as they do in Nicaragua, Angola, Ethiopia, and Mozambique (along with Tanzanian troops, who provide the same service in the Seychelles). The North Vietnamese play this role in South Vietnam, Cambodia, and Laos (although there's a report of Cuban pilots flying in the Laotian air force), while the Soviets do it themselves in Afghanistan.

Contingents of North Koreans, Libyans, and PLO Palestinians provide military training for both the army and the secret police, while various East Blockers, mostly Czechs and Bulgarians, are the technicians for a few development projects. (The 20 Czechs captured and held hostage by UNITA whom I interviewed in Angola in 1983 during a visit to Jonas Savimbi's forces were wood-pulp engineers. The irrigation pipe set up at UNITA's agricultural center near Likua was from the Bulgarian-built agricultural center at the town of Maivinga, overrun by Savimbi's men.)

The entire society is mobilized, militarized, and made to swim in a sea of Marxist propaganda. All those who object are branded as "counterrevolutionary," subject to the loss of their job or food-ration card, to harassment, being beat up, jailed, tortured, or shot.

So far, the franchise has proven quite successful and tenacious in perpetuating Soviet colonial rule. To this day, no Soviet-backed Marxist-Leninist government that has "bought" the franchise has been removed from power from within. Anwar Sadat's throwing the Soviets out of Egypt (after Nasser's death)—and perhaps even Desire Bouterse's doing the same in Surinam—may come close. (Reagan's invasion of Grenada from without, however, does not count.) But if a genuine popular rebellion from within a Soviet colony succeeds in overthrowing the ruling clique, ejecting all Soviet and Soviet-proxy personnel from the country, and establishing a democratic form of government, the doctrine of the historical inevitability of Marxism-Leninism will have been shattered.

The Pendulum of History

This is why the guerrilla wars being waged now in eight Soviet colonies on three continents represent a geopolitical phenomenon of immense historical significance. Just as the Third World rejected Western colonialism in the 1950s and '60s, so it is rejecting Soviet colonialism in the 1980s. And it is using the Soviet strategy of armed guerrilla resistance—"wars of liberation"—to do so.

This new phenomenon of *anti-Soviet liberation movements* means that one should not look at a world map and see each struggle piecemeal, but rather as all related parts of a historical momentum opposed to imperialism—the "second stage" of post-World War II nationalist movements, now aimed at Soviet Marxist imperialism.

Reprinted by permission of United Feature Syndicate, Inc.

It is, of course, an almost fantastic oversimplification to speak of the Third World as an "it," as a single entity. Nonetheless, one can argue that the pendulum of history has swung away from Soviet Marxism as a model for a great many countries in Asia, Africa, and Latin America, and towards democracy and a market economy. In Latin America, for example, Argentina, Uruguay, Venezuela, Ecuador, Peru, Colombia, Panama, Cost Rica, and Honduras are all functioning democracies, with Brazil on the way.

Destabilizing the Soviets

There is, then, a "window of opportunity" right now for freedom and democracy in the world. The Soviet Union has overexpanded and is now on the defensive. If this opportunity is not taken advantage of, the Kremlin will use this period to digest and consolidate its gains, soon to be on the imperialist march again.

United States foreign policy has long been limited to containment and defensive reaction—a genuinely *reactionary* policy that has also included propping up corrupt autocrats such as Mobutu Sese Seko in Zaire and Ferdinand Marcos in the Philippines. If the United States is to reorient its perspective from a strategic defense to a strategic offense, it must be through the development of an activist, forward-looking foreign policy with the clear-cut strategic goal of destabilizing the Soviet Union through an energetic and orchestrated exploitation of its vulnerabilities, forcefully persuading it to disarm and democratize.

Those anti-Soviet guerrillas whom I've visited and talked to— be they Nicaraguan, Afghan, Angolan, Cambodian, Laotian, Vietnamese, Mozambican, or Ethiopian—do not want US soldiers to fight for them. They want to fight for their, and their country's, own freedom. They only ask for material, diplomatic, and moral help. Given that, they will do the rest. They are handing America and the West an opportunity for permanently reducing Soviet power and influence in the world.

Evaluating Sources of Information

A critical thinker must always question sources of information. Historians, for example, usually distinguish between *primary sources (eyewitness accounts)* and *secondary sources (writings or statements based on primary or eyewitness accounts or on other secondary sources.)* A diary kept by a spy is an example of a primary account. An article by a journalist based on that diary is a secondary source.

In order to read and think critically, one must be able to recognize primary sources. However, this is not enough. Eyewitness accounts do not always provide accurate descriptions. Historians may find ten different eyewitness accounts of an event and all the accounts might interpret the event differently. The historians must then decide which of these accounts provide the most objective and accurate interpretations.

Test your skill in evaluating sources of information by completing the following exercise. Pretend that your teacher tells you to write a research report about communism's impact on Poland. You decide to include an equal number of primary and secondary sources. Listed below are a number of sources which may be useful in your research. Evaluate each of them. *Then, place a P next to those discriptions you believe are primary sources. Next, rank the primary sources assigning the number (1) to what appears to be the most objective and accurate primary source, the number (2) to the next most objective, and so on until the ranking is finished. Repeat the entire procedure, this time placing an S next to those descriptions you feel would serve as secondary sources and then ranking them.*

If you are doing this activity as a member of a class or group, discuss and compare your evaluation with other members of the group. If you are reading this book alone, you may want to ask others if they agree with your evaluation. You will probably discover that others will come to different conclusions than you. Listening to their reasons may give you valuable insights in evaluating sources of information.

P = primary
S = secondary

1. a printed interview with Lech Welesa, Solidarity leader, about the changes in civil and human rights since the communist takeover.

2. a newspaper editorial called "Poland: the Victim"

3. an article in *Pravda*, a Soviet newspaper, about cultural celebrations in Poland

4. a printed interview with a refugee from Poland telling about changing standards of living in Polish cities

5. a newspaper editorial called "Get the Commies Out of Poland"

6. a television documentary about education in Poland

7. an Australian film about a couple who escape from Poland and flee to New York City

8. an autobiography by a Polish hunger striker

9. an essay written by a leading economist about the economic effects of communism on Poland

10. film footage of rioting in Warsaw

11. a book called *The Changing Faces of Poland from 1918 to the Present*

12. excerpts from the journal of a Polish university student, executed for government opposition

13. viewpoint 1 from this chapter

14. your uncle Eddie's photos of Poland from his trip to Europe

15. an article about Poland's increasingly tough policies toward dissidents

16. an article about parliamentary elections in Poland

17. a press release from the Soviet Embassy information department reprinting a speech delivered by Mikhail Gorbachev at a Warsaw treaty organization meeting

18. a novel about a Polish student who travels to Moscow to learn about Marist-Leninist ideology

19. a printed discussion between a US ambassador to Poland and a well-known news reporter on the effectiveness of Solidarity

Bibliography

The following list of books, periodicals, and pamphlets deals with the subject matter of this chapter.

Peter L. Berger	"Underdevelopment Revisited," *Commentary*, July 1984.
Maurice R. Berube	"Assessing a Revolution: Food, Health, and Schooling in Cuba," *Commonweal*, September 6, 1985.
Economist	"Will China's Left Hand Leave Its Right Hand Free?" June 8, 1985.
Edward Gonzalez	"Exporting Revolution: Marxism in the Caribbean,"*Current*, November 1985.
Norman Gelb	"China's New Materialism," *The New Leader*, April 8, 1985.
Semou Pathe Gueye	"Marxism Is Gaining Ground in Africa," *World Marxist Review*, July 1984.
Pranay Gupte	"Third World Success Story," *Forbes*, June 18, 1984.
Irving Louis Horowitz	*Cuban Communism* (fifth edition). New Brunswick, NJ: Transaction Books, 1984.
Pico Iyer	"China: The Second Revolution," *Times*, September 23, 1985.
Dorothy E. Jones	"Capitalism in China: Under Deng Xiaoping, It's OK to Get Rich," *Business Week*, January 14, 1985.
Jonathan Kwitny	*Endless Enemies: The Making of an Unfriendly World*. New York, NY: Congdon & Weed, Inc., 1984.
Thomas J. LaBelle	"A Choice Between Capitalism, Marxism: Latin American, Caribbean Peoples Build an Indigenous Agenda," *Los Angeles Times*, March 22, 1984.
David and Marina Ottaway	*Afrocommunism*. New York, NY: Holmes & Meier Publishers, Inc., 1981.
James L. Payne	"Marxists: They Love a Man in Uniform," *Reason*, October 1985.
Ron Perrin	"Yes, But Is It Marxism?" *National Catholic Reporter*, March 29, 1985.
Donald S. Zagoria	"China's Quiet Revolution," *Foreign Affairs*, Spring 1984.

Index